The Prophet of Mercy

How Muhammad ﷺ Rose Above Enmity & Insult

MOHAMMAD ELSHINAWY
& OMAR SULEIMAN

KUBE PUBLISHING
In association with
YAQEEN™
INSTITUTE FOR ISLAMIC RESEARCH

The Prophet of Mercy:
How Muhammad ﷺ Rose Above Enmity & Insult

First published in England by
Kube Publishing Ltd
Markfield Conference Centre
Ratby Lane
Markfield
Leicestershire
LE67 9SY
United Kingdom

Tel: +44 (0) 1530 249230

Website: www.kubepublishing.com
Email: info@kubepublishing.com

Cataloguing in-Publication Data is available from the British Library

ISBN Paperback 978-1-84774-172-1
ISBN Ebook 978-1-84774-173-8
Cover design and typesetting: Jannah Haque
Printed by: IMAK Ofset, Turkey.

Transliteration

A brief guide to some of the letters and symbols used in the Arabic transliteration in this book.

th	ث	*ḥ*	ح	*dh*	ذ
ṣ	ص	*ḍ*	ض	*ṭ*	ط
ẓ	ظ	ʿ	ع	ʾ	ء

ā	ـَا ـا آ	*ī*	ـِي	*ū*	ـُو

صلى الله عليه وسلم	سبحانه وتعالى	رضي الله عنه
May the peace and blessings of Allah be upon him.	Glorified and Exalted (is He).	May Allah be pleased with him.
رضي الله عنها	رضي الله عنهما	عليه السلام
May Allah be pleased with her.	May Allah be pleased with them both.	May peace be upon him.

Contents

Introduction

In the name of Allah, the Most Compassionate, the Most Merciful.

To delegitimize the Messenger ﷺ[1] is to call into question the entire message. During his time, the Makkans called him a poet, a magician, and a madman, among other names. Today, he is insulted with other labels. Perhaps the most invidious insult, designed to undermine the powerful establishment and spread of his message, is that he overcame his foes with terror and ruled them with cruelty. Descriptions of Muhammad's life ﷺ, military career, and traditions form the foundation for most judgments about his mission. Islam as a whole, through these depictions, is seen as either a religion of peace or a religion of war, depending on which interpretation of the Messenger ﷺ and his message is followed. Modern critiques of some of the Prophet's ﷺ undertakings are meant to question the civility of Islam in the ongoing manufactured clash of civilizations that fuels both Islamophobes and extremists. Michael Bonner notes: 'Many of these modern arguments over historiography, and over the rise of Islam and the origins of jihad more generally, began in the nineteenth and the earlier twentieth centuries among European academic specialists in the study of the East, often referred to as the orientalists.'[2]

1 Honorific symbol stating: "salutations and peace be upon him".

2 Michael David, Bonner, *Jihad in Islamic History: Doctrines and Practice* (Princeton: Princeton University Press, 2006), 16.

He goes on to note that the motivation of these arguments cannot be disconnected from 'their involvement in the colonial project'.[3]

By portraying the Prophet ﷺ himself as a barbarian, surely his followers must also be treated as an inherently violent political body that will employ any means necessary to achieve global domination. What is uncontroversial is that Muhammad ﷺ succeeded at wielding unprecedented power even after decades of persecution. Michael Hart, who famously considered him the most influential man in history, wrote:

> My choice of Muhammad to lead the list of the world's most influential persons may surprise some readers and may be questioned by others, but he was the only man in history who was supremely successful on both the religious and secular level.[4]

The question of whether or not he sacrificed his principles in the pursuit of that success is one that requires an in-depth look at his consistency, or lack thereof, in varied political contexts.

---

3 Ibid.

4 Michael H., Hart, *The 100: A Ranking of the Most Influential Persons in History* (New York: Hart Pub. Co., 1978), 21.

'His Character ﷺ 'Was the Qur'an'

This was the description of the Prophet ﷺ given by 'Ā'ishah ﷺ. He practiced everything he preached. He was an embodiment of the message; all the verses of grace, ethics, and beauty were embodied in his example. Allah says, *'Repel that which is evil with that which is better'* (*Fuṣṣilat* 41:34), and it is in his example that we find how to rise above every form of evil one may face, particularly at the hands of those who show us hostility. The 'evil' is relative—and so is the response. Therefore, each unique circumstance that the Prophet ﷺ faced required a different response. The consistency with which he adopted the noblest course in every situation is what stands out and makes him venerable. Islamophobes argue that Muhammad ﷺ was himself the author of the Qur'an; hence, the Qur'an became less tolerant as his power grew. Muslims argue that the Prophet ﷺ was the embodiment of the Qur'an, which is the word of Allah, and that both his character and the prose of the Qur'an were consistent in their grace. The verses of battle were revealed only post-Madinah because the battles did not take place until the Prophet ﷺ had assumed the role of a head of state. Yet, some of the most prominent verses of tolerance, such as the verse: *'There is no compulsion in religion'* (*al-Baqarah* 2:256), were also revealed post-Madinah.

A Blessing in Disguise

As we immerse ourselves in how the Prophet Muhammad ﷺ magnanimously treated his enemies, how graciously he responded to decades of aggression, and how he unfailingly transcended insults and injuries, we come to a number of stark realizations. One of which is how Islamophobia and its associated fear-mongering are truly blessings in disguise. The torrential downpour of allegations about Allah's Messenger ﷺ using violence to force conversions,[5] or being an unprincipled opportunist,[6] are ultimately forcing us to rediscover his character anew.

Any impartial reader of the Prophet's ﷺ biography will quickly discover which 'snapshots' taken from his life are dishonest in their representation, which were depictions of his normative practices, and which were exceptions to the norm. In fact, as one reads further, one realizes that even these 'exceptions' were not trivial hiccups in his character, but rather another dimension of his superior persona and universal mercy that many simply fail to understand.

5 Attributed to Manuel II Palaiologos, a 14th century Byzantine emperor, but more recently quoted by Pope Benedict XVI, 'Show me just what Muhammad brought that was new and there you will find things only evil and inhumane, such as his command to spread by the sword the faith he preached.' Lecture of the Holy Father–Faith, Reason and the University Memories and Reflections, *Libreria Editrice Vaticana*, 12 September 2006.

6 Throughout her writings, Ayaan Hirsi Ali argues that many Muslims today understand from the life of Prophet Muhammad ﷺ that imposing their religion on others is a requirement of their faith, and the moment he ﷺ fled to Madinah and 'cobbled together a militia', his true colours surfaced. See: 'Islam is a Religion of Violence', *Foreign Policy*, 9 November 2015.

The following pages serve to start readers on that journey, lifting them above superficial information and manipulative illustrations of the Prophet Muhammad ﷺ, whom Almighty God described as *'a mercy to the worlds'* (*al-Anbiyā'* 21:107), and *'upon an exalted [standard] of character'* (*al-Qalam* 68:4).

We have compiled seventy incidents in which the Prophet ﷺ rose above enmity and insult. Before addressing the three or four incidents employed by those who wish to portray him as a violent opportunist, it is crucial to shed light on the overwhelming number of incidents that characterize his dealings, political or otherwise. Each incident has been paraphrased for the sake of brevity, but references to the original narrations are provided as source material for those who wish to extract further benefit from these incidents.

The primary goal is to form a foundation for understanding how the Prophet ﷺ consistently showed honour and nobility when insulted and attacked. It is only with this background that incidents that appear to be exceptions to this rule can be accurately analysed. Another goal of this collection is to inspire the followers of Muhammad ﷺ to demonstrate mercy and benevolence in the face of insult, just as their Prophet ﷺ did. Surely, all of the cruelty and bigotry hurled at the followers of Muhammad ﷺ today pales in comparison to the vicious attacks he endured in life. Just as it hurts us to see him insulted, it would pain him to see us responding in ways insulting to his legacy.

A Difficult Decade in Makkah

Once the Prophet Muhammad ﷺ began to preach Islam publicly, his few followers quickly found that merely professing faith meant facing ruthless torture and even execution. Men from the Makkan nobility, like Abū Bakr ؓ, were beaten unconscious in the streets while slaves like Bilāl ibn Rabāḥ ؓ and Ṣuhayb ibn Sinān ؓ were shackled and left to scorch in the midday desert Sun. The first martyr was Sumayyah bint Khayyāṭ ؓ, who was murdered with a spear thrust through her pelvis, and her son, ʿAmmār ibn Yāsir ؓ, was tortured with fire—like so many others—until he verbally feigned recanting his faith.[7] Khabbāb ibn al-Aratt ؓ was forced to lie on burning coals and smell his own flesh cooking,[8] and some of these atrocities only escalated as this tragic decade progressed.

As for the Prophet ﷺ himself, the abuse he suffered from the idolaters of the Quraysh was brutal. They spared no opportunity to demonize him, divorced his daughters, and exiled and starved his entire clan for three years. As for physical assault, ʿUqbah ibn Abī Muʿayt strangled him from behind when he prayed in public, Abū Jahl ordered camel intestines to be dumped over him while he prostrated, ʿUtaybah ibn Abī Lahab spat at him, and others beat him unconscious.

A number of key observations can be noted from the period of persecution. Muhammad ﷺ clearly directed a policy of

---

7 See: *Mustadrak al-Ḥākim; Bāb at-Tafsīr; Sūrah an-Nahl; Illā Man Ukriha wa Qalbuhu Mutma'inn bil-Īmān.*

8 See: *Sunan Ibn Mājah* (153) and *Ḥilyat al-Awliyā'* (472).

perseverance and non-violent response against a backdrop of repeated provocations of the Quraysh. These provocations increased in severity as the Quraysh grew frustrated at their failure to stop his preaching; he had an eager and receptive audience that grew steadily despite all efforts to instil fear in it. Abū Lahab, one of his paternal uncles, began to hurl insults at him from the moment he started preaching to his own clan members from the mount of Ṣafā near the Kaʿbah, a place commonly used to address the people.[9] This incident paved the way for public mocking of Muslims to become the norm, particularly when they were seen praying at the Kaʿbah.[10]

> *Warn your nearest kinfolk and lower your wing tenderly over the believers who follow you. If they disobey you, say, 'I bear no responsibility for your actions.' Put your trust in the Almighty, the Merciful, who sees you when you stand up [for prayer] and sees your movements among the worshippers: He is the All-Hearing, the All-Knowing.* (*ash-Shuʿarā'* 26:214–220)[11]

A concerted effort was made by the Quraysh—who viewed the Muslims as rebellious criminals for abandoning the pagan religion of their forefathers—to prevent anyone they could from listening to Muhammad ﷺ. This was true both within and outside Makkah, as people from across the Arabian Peninsula who frequented Makkah for worship and trade began to come in contact with him and the Message of Islam.

---

9 Ghazālī, *Fiqh-us-Sīrah: Understanding the Life of Prophet Muhammad*, 117.

10 Ṣallābī, *The Noble Life of the Prophet* ﷺ, 327.

11 Haleem, *The Qur'an: A New Translation by M.A.S. Abdel Haleem*, 237.

Walīd ibn al-Mughīrah, an elite Makkan and highly influential businessman, initiated a smear campaign against Muhammad ﷺ at a council of tribal leaders. In it, he devised a plan to accuse Muhammad ﷺ of being a magician as a way to warn the public against the mesmerizing effect his words had on those who heard him recite the Qur'an.[12] Historical incidents of additional propaganda efforts accusing him of being a liar, a madman, being possessed, and a poet who lured and manipulated people into following him, are also recorded in the Qur'an.[13]

> *The disbelievers almost strike you down with their looks when they hear the Qur'an. They say, 'He must be mad!'* (*al-Qalam* 68:51)

> *The disbelievers think it strange that a prophet of their own people has come to warn them: they say, 'He is just a lying sorcerer.'* (*Ṣād* 38:4)

Pained by the visible suffering of his followers and unable to protect them from harm, Muhammad ﷺ was at the same time aggrieved at not being able to convince the community at large—many of whom were his own clan members. Despite this, his strategy was a deliberate one: to continue to invite people, choosing to appeal to their sense of morality and reason over the potentially far more destructive use of force.

---

12 Ghazālī, *Fiqh-us-Sīrah: Understanding the Life of Prophet Muhammad*, 125.

13 Ibid, 121.

When seen through the lens of a tribal society, any one of the provocations of the Quraysh would have been sufficient cause for war between the tribes involved. Yet, we see unprecedented individual and collective self-control, conviction, and perseverance that can only be realized with great spiritual and moral foresight; this foresight was the foundation of a leadership strategy for reform that Muhammad ﷺ was carefully building at this stage in Makkah. This came at a time in which he and his followers had not been given divine permission to take up arms—even as a means of defence. As the Muslims were a minority living in a city largely hostile towards them, war would have destroyed the few who had joined the ranks of the Muslims, as well as any chance of establishing this fledgling community.

In light of the tribal system the Quraysh were accustomed to, it was not easy to simply go to battle against the Muslims, given that Muhammad ﷺ and his followers were not from any one clan alone, and several among them were the youth of the most elite and powerful tribes—and therefore under protection. Rather, war at this stage would have necessitated large-scale participation across many clans, even against those with whom alliances existed, and, potentially, against one's own family members. As al-Ṣallābi notes: 'As the matter stood, Islam spread throughout all of the Quraysh's clans, without any of the adverse effects that result from tribal loyalty.'[14]

14 Ṣallābi, *The Noble Life of the Prophet (peace be upon him)*, 181.

Ultimately, the Prophet Muhammad ﷺ fled this persecution by migrating with his Companions to Madinah, but not before leaving in the pages of history a matchless legacy of forgiveness and dignified dealings with one's enemies. In this book, we explore a few of these remarkable instances from humanity's most luminous life ever.

1 Let the Angels Respond

Despite the Qur'an affirming that the insults of the Quraysh[15] tightened his chest with pain, he never stooped to reciprocating in kind. In fact, he inevitably took the higher road of not responding at all, hopeful that this would one day penetrate their harsh hearts, following Allah's injunction to: *'Repel [evil] by that [deed] which is better; and thereupon the one whom between you and him is enmity [will become] as though he was a devoted friend'* (*Fuṣṣilat* 41:34).

On one occasion, the Prophet ﷺ silently smiled when Abū Bakr ؓ, his noblest Companion, refrained from responding to a person who was insulting him. But when Abū Bakr ؓ eventually spoke up, the Prophet ﷺ became angry and left. He later explained: 'An angel was with you, responding on your behalf. But when you said back to him some of what he said, a devil arrived, and it is not for me to sit with devils.'[16] The Prophet thereby ﷺ taught that when a person stoops to the level of those who insult them, they allow the devil to steer their course. One of the core principles of Islamic spirituality is

15 The Quraysh would call the Prophet Muhammad ﷺ insane, a sorcerer, a soothsayer, a fraud (plagiarizer), a mere poet, barren (unmanly), cursed by the gods, and other such insults.

16 Collected by Ahmad (9251) and Abū Dāwūd (4896), and al-Arna'oot deemed it *ḥasan li-ghayrih* (sound in light of its corroborating chains).

to not allow our emotions and actions to be hijacked by the devil to the point where our decision-making is driven by anything other than divine instruction.

The Prophet ﷺ taught various methods such as seeking refuge in Allah from the devil, changing our physical positions to less confrontational ones and performing ablution, amongst others, to help us maintain our composure when angry. In anger, we tend to respond in prideful, satanic ways that serve nothing and no one but our own egos. Righteous anger is necessary, but cannot be expressed when one is not appropriately composed. Therefore, the Prophet ﷺ overcame any attempts on the part of his enemies to provoke foulness, vulgarity, or anything not befitting his noble character.

2 They Are Misguided in Their Insults

Arwā bint Ḥarb—also known as Um Jameel, the wife of Abū Lahab—would follow the Prophet ﷺ around to hurt and humiliate him and used to taunt him, 'The dispraised (Mudhammam) we have denied, and his religion we have loathed, and his command we have defied (مُذَمَّمٌ أَبَيْنَا وَدِينَهُ قَلَيْنَا وَأَمْرُهُ عَصَيْنَا)!' Instead of responding to her, he would simply find solace in saying to his Companions: 'Don't you see how Allah diverts from me the curses and insults of the Quraysh? They insult Mudhammam, and they curse Mudhammam, while I am Muhammad (The Praised One)!'[17]

The situation was quickly calmed by the Prophet finding optimism at a time where it seemed impossible to detect a silver lining. We, too, should see that the cartoons and drawings that people claim to be his likeness are in fact far removed from our beloved Prophet ﷺ.

[17] Collected by al-Bukhārī (334).

3 Praying for Guidance and Recognizing Their Potential

ʿAmr ibn Hishām (more famously known as Abū Jahl) was his staunchest enemy—the pharaoh of his nation. Despite inflicting physical and emotional wounds on the Messenger of Allah ﷺ, and despite breaking his Companions' bones and later leading the first army against them, he ﷺ still prayed for his guidance. He ﷺ used to say in Makkah, "O Allah, strengthen Islam with Abū Jahl ibn Hishām or ʿUmar ibn al-Khaṭṭāb." The following morning, ʿUmar ibn al-Khaṭṭāb embraced Islam.[18] Despite Abū Jahl being the pharaoh of the Muslims, the Prophet ﷺ had the heart to pray for him, and the judgment to see his promising leadership qualities that could potentially be used for good.

18 Collected by at-Tirmidhī (3683).

4 Sparing Them Divine Punishment

When the Quraysh became even more vicious, the Prophet ﷺ prayed, 'O Allah, send years [of famine] upon them like the seven years [of famine during the time] of Joseph.' As a result, a famine overtook them like that of Prophet Joseph's time ﷺ, destroying every kind of life and forcing people to eat hides and carcasses to the point that they hallucinated seeing smoke. Abū Sufyān came to the Prophet ﷺ and said, 'O Muhammad, you order people to obey Allah and keep good relations with their kin. The people of your tribe are dying, so please pray to Allah for them.'

Ultimately, the Prophet ﷺ received verses from The Smoke (*Sūrah ad-Dukhān*) and he supplicated for them. A cloud quickly appeared and poured forth rain in abundance, and he supplicated for them *again* when they subsequently complained of the excessive rain. But once they were quenched and secure, they soon relapsed into rejection and rebellion.[19]

[19] Collected by al-Bukhārī (133, 333).

5 Showing Mercy on the Worst Day of His Life

It was repoted by ʿĀ'ishah ﵂ that she once asked the Prophet ﷺ: 'Have you encountered a day harder than the Day of Uḥud?' The Prophet ﷺ said:

> Your tribe has abused me much, and the worst was the day of ʿAqabah when I presented myself to ʿAbd Yalīl ibn ʿAbd Kulāl, and he did not respond to what I sought. I departed, overwhelmed with grief, and I could not relax until I found myself at a tree where I lifted my head towards the sky to see a cloud shading me. I looked up and saw Gabriel in it. He called out to me, saying, 'Allah has heard your people's saying to you and how they have replied, and Allah has sent the Angel of the Mountains to you that you may order him to do whatever you wish to these people.' The Angel of the Mountains greeted me and said, 'O Muhammad, order what you wish, and if you like, I will let the two mountains fall upon them.' I said, 'No. Rather, I hope that Allah will bring from their descendants people who will worship Allah alone without associating partners with Him.'[20]

In other reports, he spent ten days in Ṭā'if after speaking to its leaders, calling its people to Islam, until mobs gathered to

[20] Collected by al-Bukhārī (3059) and Muslim (1795).

drive him out. They made two rows and forced him through them while they hurled obscenities and pelted stones until blood ran down his blessed legs, and Zayd ibn Ḥārithah's head was gashed.[21]

21 Collected by Ibn Hishām in *as-Sīrah* (2/70–72) and Ibn Saʿd in *at-Tabaqāt al-Kubrā* (1/211–221).

6 More Hope in a Tribe Than Its Own Chief

When Ṭufayl ibn ʿAmr ad-Dawsī رضي الله عنه first visited Makkah he was fearful of being bewitched by the Prophet ﷺ and even placed cotton in his ears while circling the Kaʿbah. Nevertheless, he embraced Islam shortly thereafter. When he carried this message back to his people, however, they shunned him and adamantly refused. Abū Hurayrah رضي الله عنه reports that Ṭufayl ibn ʿAmr رضي الله عنه then travelled back to the Prophet ﷺ and said: 'O Messenger of Allah, Daws has defied [your call] so invoke Allah against them.' The Prophet ﷺ said: 'O Allah, guide Daws and bring them forth [as Muslims].'[22] Nearly a decade later, Ṭufayl ibn ʿAmr رضي الله عنه migrated with eighty families—now Muslims—to Madinah.

22 Collected by al-Bukhārī (4131).

7 Maintaining the Trust of His Persecutors

When the Messenger of Allah ﷺ migrated from Makkah, he took many of his persecutors' belongings with him for safekeeping. His integrity was never compromised, even though these individuals had expelled his Companions and subjected them to persecution. 'Ā'ishah ؓ said:

> He ﷺ instructed 'Alī ؓ to stay behind in Makkah in order to return all the trust the Messenger of Allah ﷺ held for people. There was nobody in Makkah—even his enemies—who had valuables except that he kept them with the Messenger of Allah ﷺ due to the honesty and trustworthiness that was known [to all] about him. Thus, 'Alī ؓ stayed back for three days and three nights to deliver everything entrusted by the people to the Messenger of Allah ﷺ back to them, and then caught up with him after completing that task.[23]

[23] Collected by al-Bayhaqī in *as-Sunan al-Kubrā* (12477), Ibn Kathīr ibn *al-Bidāyah wan-Nihāyah* (3/218–219), and at-Ṭabarī in *Tārīkh al-Umam wal-Mulūk* (2/372).

8 Integrity in a Desperate Situation

Surāqah ibn Mālik ﵁ was one of the bounty hunters in hot pursuit of the Prophet ﷺ during his migration to Madinah. When Surāqah tracked them down, Abū Bakr ﵁ began weeping out of fear for the Prophet ﷺ, while the Messenger of Allah ﷺ prayed, 'O Allah, suffice us regarding them however You wish.' The legs of Surāqah's horse sank deep into the firm earth so far that it reached the horse's stomach. Surāqah leapt off his mount and said:

> O Muhammad, I have become certain that this is your doing, so ask Allah to rescue me from what I am in. By Allah, I will blind those [chasing] after you from [knowing] your whereabouts. And here is my quiver, take an arrow from it, and when you come across my camels and sheep in such-and-such a place, take from them whatever you like.

The Messenger of Allah ﷺ said, 'I have no need for them', and supplicated until Surāqah was released and returned to his people.[24]

[24] Collected by al-Bukhārī (3419) and Muslim (2009), and this is the wording of Aḥmad (17627) about which al-Arna'oot said, 'Its chain is authentic according to the criteria of [Imam] Muslim.'

The Legacy Continues in Madinah

The Prophet ﷺ actively solicited followers from other tribes to grant him protection from his persecutors. The people of Yathrib—now Madinah—responded, and they secretly met the Prophet ﷺ during the season of pilgrimage in Makkah. It was during this meeting that they took a pledge with him and suggested that they attack the unsuspecting Makkans at night. Muhammad ﷺ refused, saying it was unbefitting his message. Muhammad's ﷺ refusal to take up arms against the ruling class in Makkah frustrated even some of his staunchest followers. Khabbāb ibn al-Aratt, who was amongst those most severely tortured for accepting Islam, said:

> We complained to Allah's Messenger of the persecution inflicted on us while he was sitting in the shade of the Kaʿbah, leaning over his cloak. We said to him, 'Would you seek help for us? Would you pray to Allah for us?' He said, 'Among the nations before you a believing man would be put in a ditch that was dug for him, and a saw would be put over his head and he would be cut into two pieces, yet that torture would not make him give up his religion. His body would be combed with iron combs that would remove his flesh from the bones and nerves, yet that would not make him abandon his religion. By Allah, this religion will prevail in a way that a traveller from Sana to Hadramaut will fear none but Allah, and a sheep will not fear the attack of a wolf, but you people are hasty!'[25]

[25] Muḥammad Ibn Ismāʿīl Bukhārī and Muhammad Muhsin Khan. *Ṣaḥīḥ al-Bukhārī: The Translation of the Meanings of Saḥīḥ Al-Bukhari: Arabic-English*. (Riyadh-Saudi Arabia: Darussalam Pub. & Distr., 1997), Hadith 3612.

It is interesting to note that Muhammad ﷺ never made guarantees to his followers of any material incentive for supporting him. He promised them only the rewards of the afterlife. The loyalty that he garnered from a few followers who experienced no worldly benefit for following him was so strong that they became known for never fleeing the battlefield.[26]

He fled the persecution of Makkah and was invited to govern in the city of Madinah. He went from fugitive to governor practically overnight and adjusted his strategies accordingly.

This migration (hijrah) marked a turning point in Muhammad's fortunes and a new stage in the history of the Islamic movement. Islam took on a political form with the establishment of an Islamic community-state in Madinah. The importance of the hijrah is reflected in its adoption as the beginning of the Islamic calendar. In Madinah, Muhammad had the opportunity to implement God's governance and message, for he was now the prophet-head of a religiopolitical community. He did this by establishing his leadership in Madinah, subduing Makkah, and consolidating Muslim rule over the remainder of Arabia through diplomatic and military means. Muhammad had come to Madinah as the arbiter or judge for the entire community, Muslim and non-Muslim alike.[27]

---

[26] Zeitlin, *The Historical Muhammad*, 317.

[27] Esposito, John L. *Islam: The Straight Path*. Revised Third ed. New York: Oxford University Press, 2005. pp. 8–9.

Far from enacting a policy of vengeance and intolerance, the Prophet ﷺ implemented a system of mercy that was in direct opposition to the cruelty he and his followers had been subjected to in Makkah.

9 Refusal to Resort to Name Calling

Abdullāh ibn Ubayy—also known as Ibn Salūl—was the head of the hypocrites in Madinah, and schemed non-stop to undermine the Prophet's authority and influence ﷺ. Soon after the Messenger of Allah ﷺ arrived, he ﷺ rode past a group including Ibn Salūl and began inviting them to Islam. Ibn Salūl rudely retorted, 'Stay in your home. If someone would like to hear your message, they will come to you.' In another narration, 'Now leave, the smell of your donkey bothers us.' The Muslims became irate upon hearing these insults, but the Prophet ﷺ forbade them from retaliating.

Later, he complained to Saʿd ibn ʿUbādah ﷺ and said, 'Did you hear what Abū Ḥubāb said?'—calling Ibn Salūl by his epithet of respect (*kunyah*) even behind closed doors! Saʿd ﷺ urged the Messenger of Allah ﷺ to forgive him, explaining, 'God sent you as they were finalizing the crown with jewels for him to reign as king over Madinah, but Allah destined otherwise, and thus he fumes with envy.'[28] He did forgive him, and continued to forgive him on numerous subsequent occasions as well.

[28] Collected by al-Bukhārī (856) and Muslim (4431).

10 God Loves Gentleness

In Madinah, a group of people from a Jewish tribe entered upon the Prophet ﷺ and said, '*As-Sāmmu 'alayk* (Death be upon you).' He replied, 'And upon you', but 'Ā'ishah ﵂ felt compelled to add: 'Death be upon you, along with the curse of Allah and His wrath!' The Messenger of Allah ﷺ said, 'O 'Ā'ishah, be gentle! Indeed, Allah is Gentle and loves gentleness in all matters. Beware of being harsh and vulgar.' She said, 'Did you not hear what they said?' He replied, 'Did you not hear how I replied? I have returned their statement to them, except that my invocation against them will be accepted, while theirs against me will not be accepted.'[29]

Remarkably, even being in a position of power did not tempt him to retaliate or repeat back the same words; he did not even let his wife respond harshly to those who insulted him.

[29] Collected by al-Bukhārī (410, 6528).

11 Abuse Only Increased Him in Grace

Zayd ibn Suʿnah ؓ was a great Jewish Rabbi of Madinah. When Allah wished to guide him, Zayd thought of testing the Prophet ﷺ by lending him eighty *mithqāl* (350 grams) of gold for a fixed period. A few days before repayment was due, Zayd grabbed the Messenger of Allah ﷺ angrily by his cloak, in front of all the senior Companions, and said, 'O Muhammad, why are you not paying what is due? By Allah, I know your family well! You are all known for deferring your debts!' The Prophet ﷺ said to the infuriated ʿUmar who threatened to kill Zayd for his disrespect, 'O ʿUmar, we do not need this… Go with him, pay off his loan, and give him twenty additional *sāʿ* (thirty-two kilograms) of dates because you frightened him.' It was that response that convinced Zayd ibn Suʿnah to embrace Islam.

He explained to ʿUmar:

> There was not a single sign of prophethood except that I recognized it upon looking at Muhammad's face—except for two that I had not yet seen from him: that his tolerance overcomes his anger, and that intense abuse only increases him in forbearance. I have now tested these, so know, O ʿUmar, that I accept Allah as [my] Lord, Islam as [my] religion,

Muhammad as [my] Prophet, and that half my wealth—for I have much wealth—is a donation for the ummah of Muhammad ﷺ.[30]

30 Collected by Ibn Ḥibbān (288), al-Bayhaqī (11066) and al-Ḥākim (6547) who said, 'This Hadith has an authentic chain, though they (al-Bukhārī and Muslim) did not collect it.' Al-Haythami said in *Majma' az-Zawā'id*, 'Ibn Mājah collected a part of it, and it was narrated [entirely] by at-Ṭabarānī via narrators that are [all] trustworthy.'

12 The Quraysh's Scout

On route to Badr, the Muslims were able to apprehend the Quraysh's war-scout and bring him back to the Prophet ﷺ. When the Companions began roughing up this man as they interrogated him for vital information, the Prophet ﷺ hastened to finish his *ṣalāh* and said, 'You beat him when he is honest with you, and you leave him be when he lies to you?'[31] Despite the fact that this person belonged to an opposing army, and that torture might reveal critical information about the enemy's points of weakness, he ﷺ still intervened. Thus, when Imām Mālik رحمه الله was asked, 'Can a captive be tortured if it is hoped that he can reveal the enemy's points of vulnerability?' he said, 'We have never heard of this [in our tradition].'[32]

31 Collected by Ibn Ibn Hishām (1/616–617), as-Ṣāliḥī ash-Shāmī in *Subul al-Hudā war-Rashād* (4/27), and as-Suhaylī in *ar-Rawḍ al-'Unf* (3/58).

32 See: *at-Tāj al-Ikhlīl* (3/353).

13 Maintain Your Promise

Prior to the Battle of Badr, Ḥudhayfah ibn al-Yamān ﵁ came to the Prophet ﷺ with an ethical dilemma. The Quraysh had just freed him and his father on the condition that he would not fight the Quraysh alongside the Messenger of Allah ﷺ. Despite the Muslim army being disadvantaged and about to face an army three times its size, the Prophet ﷺ said, 'Then go [to Madinah]. We will keep our promise to them, and we will seek aid from Allah against them.'[33]

His prophetic morals did not allow him, even in an extremely vulnerable position, to compromise his principles.

[33] Collected by Muslim (1787).

14 I will not Mutilate Him, Lest Allah Mutilate Me

Following the Battle of Badr, the Muslims found Suhayl ibn ʿAmr—a chief of the Quraysh and a vocal adversary of Islam—among the prisoners of war. ʿUmar ؓ was delighted at a chance to exact revenge, and requested permission to remove Suhayl's front teeth 'so that he could never preach against the Messenger ﷺ.' However, the Prophet Muhammad ﷺ said, 'I will not mutilate him, lest Allah mutilate me—even though I am a Prophet.'[34] Over a millennium before any international conventions or charters, the Prophet of Mercy ﷺ established that prisoners of war were entitled to humane treatment. This was 1,300 years before the signatories at Geneva defined humane treatment of prisoners. Compare this tradition with that of multiple methods of physical and psychological torture in prisons today. Furthermore, Muhammad ﷺ highlighted through his statement that no authority—not even a prophet—would escape accountability for torturing those under their care.

[34] Collected by al-Ḥākim (3/318) and Ibn Hishām (3/200).

15 Merciful Instincts

Although 'Umar رضي الله عنه urged him to execute the captives of Badr, and before revelation corrected the Prophet's ﷺ decision to spare these war criminals, the Messenger of Allah ﷺ was inclined to spare them—presuming this to be the greater good.[35] In fact, he emphasized to his Companions after Badr, 'Treat the captives well.'[36] This was despite the fact that those captives had specifically intended to assassinate him and had prepared to celebrate over his corpse with wine.

[35] Collected by Muslim (1763).

[36] Collected by at-Ṭabarānī in *al-Kabīr* (977), and in *as-Ṣaghīr* (409), and al-Haythamī said in *Majma' az-Zawā'id* (6/115), its chain is sound (*ḥasan*).

16 Feeding the Captives

Allah says, *'And they feed with their own food, despite their love [for it], the needy, the orphan, and the captive'* (*al-Insān* 76:8). Here, Allah informs Muslims that feeding prisoners is a means of nearness to Him, and that one should provide the food one loves—not food of inferior quality, or after satiating one's own hunger first. We are told by the Prophet ﷺ that a woman who kept a cat captive without feeding it would enter the Fire.[37] Ibn 'Abbās ؓ said, 'On the Day of Badr, the Messenger of Allah ﷺ instructed us to honor the captives, and so we gave them precedence over ourselves at mealtimes.'[38] Zurārah ibn 'Umayr (also known as Abū 'Azīz), a pagan brother of Mus'ab ibn 'Umayr, who the Muslims had captured at Badr, said, 'They used to single me out with the bread, while they would just eat dates, due to the entrustment of Allah's Messenger ﷺ.'[39] Understandably, Abū 'Azīz did not forget this unexpected treatment, and it must have influenced his eventual decision to embrace Islam.

---

37 Collected by al-Bukhārī (3482) and Muslim (2242).

38 This was also stated by Sa'īd ibn Jubayr, 'Aṭā' ibn Abī Rabāh, al-Ḥasan al-Baṣrī, and Qatādah. See: *Tafsīr Ibn Kathīr* (4/584).

39 See: *as-Sīrah* (2/475) by Ibn Kathīr and *at-Tabaqāt al-Kubrā* (2/15) by Ibn Sa'd.

17 Clothing the Captives

In a chapter titled 'Clothing the Captives', Imam al-Bukhārī narrates in his *Saḥīḥ* from Jābir ibn 'Abdillāh ؓ, who said:

> On the Day of Badr, the captives were brought, and brought [with them] was al-'Abbās ؓ who had no garment on him. The Prophet ﷺ had them find a shirt for him, and they found that only the shirt of 'Abdullāh ibn Ubayy (who was also tall) fit him, so the Prophet ﷺ clothed him with it.[40]

Later in the Prophet's life ﷺ, he even sent a man to Makkah to purchase a specific type of cloak for the captives from Hawāzin.[41]

40 Collected by al-Bukhārī (2846) and al-Bayhaqī in *as-Sunan al-Kubrā* (18570).

41 Collected by al-Bayhaqī in *Dalā'il an-Nubuwwa* (5/264).

18 Lenience With the Ransom

The Prophet Muhammad ﷺ even took his enemy prisoners' economic status into consideration when granting them opportunities for freedom. For wealthy prisoners like Abū Wadāʿah and Zurārah ibn ʿUmar, he took the full 4,000 dirhams while poorer prisoners paid only 40 *uqiyyah* (1,600 dirhams).[42] In fact, some were freed without any ransom at all, such as al-Muṭṭalib ibn Ḥanṭab, Abū ʿIzzah (the poet), Abū al-ʿĀs ibn ar-Rābīʿ, and Sayfī ibn Abī Rifāʿah.[43]

42 See: *at-Tabaqāt* (4/14) by Ibn Saʿd.

43 See: *ʿUyoon al-Athar* (1/352) by Ibn Sayyid an-Nās.

19 Increased Opportunities for Freedom

'Ibn 'Abbās رضي الله عنهما said, 'There were people from the captives at Badr who had no [money] to ransom themselves, so the Messenger of Allah ﷺ declared their ransom to be teaching [literacy] to the children of the Anṣār.'[44] Clearly one bent on vengeance or riches would never provide such a variety of avenues for criminals to return to their families and mend their deviant ways. Furthermore, the practice of freeing literate captives for teaching people how to read was unprecedented. This highlights the emphasis of the Prophet ﷺ and his message on education as a means of light and advancement.

44 Collected by Ahmad (2216), and al-Arna'oot said, 'This chain of transmission is *ḥasan*.' In *Majma' az-Zawā'id* (4/172), al-Haythami said, 'It was collected by Aḥmad from 'Alī ibn 'Āṣim who makes many mistakes, though Ahmad deemed him trustworthy.'

20 Introducing Prisoner Exchange

For various reasons, the people of Arabia had rarely engaged in prisoner exchange, but the Prophet Muhammad ﷺ made this practice common. It suffices to mention that the Muslims handed over ʿAmr ibn Abī Sufyān for the release of Saʿd ibn an-Nuʿmān ibn Akāl, even though the latter was not a prisoner of war, but rather just an innocent man who had been kidnapped by al-ʿAbbās while performing *ʿumrah* in Makkah.[45] The Prophet ﷺ replaced the practice of mutilating captives as a deterrent to continued hostilities with the far more humane practice of prisoner exchange.

[45] See: *al-Bidāyah wan-Nihāyah* (3/311) by Ibn Kathīr.

21 Keeping Captive Families Together

The Messenger of Allah ﷺ even cared about the emotional well-being of the captive; he used to provide detailed instructions on how to treat parents and children humanely by keeping them together. Abū Ayyūb ؓ reports that he heard the Messenger of Allah ﷺ say, 'Whoever separates a mother and her child, Allah will separate him and his loved ones on the Day of Resurrection.'[46]

When Abū Usayd ('Abdullāh ibn Thābit) al-Anṣārī ؓ brought captives from Bahrain, they were lined up in ranks. The Messenger of Allah ﷺ stood to see them, and he found a woman crying in their midst. He said, 'What makes you cry?' She said, 'My son was sold to Banū 'Abs.' The Messenger of Allah ﷺ said to Abū Usayd, 'You must ride out and bring him!' Abū Usayd responded immediately by riding out to retrieve the child and reunite him with his mother.[47]

---

[46] Collected by at-Tirmidhī (1566) who called it *ḥasan-gharīb*, Ahmad (23546) and al-Arna'oot called it collectively *ḥasan* in light of its corroborating chains. It was also narrated by al-Ḥākim (2334) who deemed it authentic according to the criteria of Muslim, and aṭ-Ṭabarānī in *al-Kabīr* (4080), al-Bayhaqī in *al-Kubrā* (18089), and al-Albani deemed it authentic in *Saheeh al-Jāmi'* (6412).

[47] Collected by al-Ḥākim (6193) who said, 'This *Hadith* has an authentic chain, though they (al-Bukhārī and Muslim) did not collect it.' It was also collected by Sa'īd ibn Manṣūr in *as-Sunan* (2654).

22 No Favour Forgotten

Following the Battle of Badr, he ﷺ said, 'Were al-Muṭʿīm ibn ʿAdī still alive, and he spoke to me regarding these foul men, I would have freed them [all] for him!'[48] Ibn ʿAdī was not a believer, but he had not only helped to destroy the Quraysh's pact to boycott Banū Hāshim but he had also granted the Prophet ﷺ asylum upon his return from Ṭā'if. The Prophet ﷺ demonstrated loyalty and gratitude to anyone who had helped him in his time of need, regardless of whether or not they chose to accept his Prophetic mission.

48 Collected by al-Bukhārī (2970), Abū Dāwūd (2689), at-Ṭabarānī in *al-Kabeer* (1/302), and Ibn Athīr in *Asad al-Ghābah* (1/337).

23 Averting War With Banū Qaynuqāʿ

Upon returning to Madinah from the Battle of Badr, the tribe of Banū Qaynuqāʿ threatened the Prophet ﷺ and his Companions, saying, 'Do not be deluded by your triumph against some amateur fighters who have no experience in battle. If you were to fight against us, you would come to know that we are the true warriors, and that you have never faced anyone like us.'[49] This was one of the final vexations after two years of publicly mocking Allah and His Messenger ﷺ and instigating hostilities between the Muslims.

Some also report that a craftsman from Banū Qaynuqāʿ undressed a Muslim woman in the marketplace and was killed for it by a Muslim who heard her scream. Banū Qaynuqāʿ gathered and killed that man in retaliation. When the Prophet ﷺ eventually decided to march against them, 'Abdullāh ibn Ubayy physically restrained him by grabbing onto his armour and insisting that he abort this campaign. The Prophet ﷺ became very angry and demanded that Ibn Ubayy let him go, but he would not. He kept pleading that Banū Qaynuqāʿ were his allies, and that he feared vulnerability without them. In the end, the Prophet ﷺ said, 'I have released them for you', and allowed the entire tribe to leave Madinah unharmed, and to take whatever they owned except for their weapons.[50]

49 Collected by Abū Dāwūd (3001).

50 See: *as-Sīrah* (2/48) by Ibn Hishām with a sound *mursal* chain.

24 They Just Don't Know Any Better

In the second major battle (Uḥud) against the Muslims, the Quraysh's army—this time 3,000 strong against the Muslims' 700—managed to ambush the Prophet ﷺ. His front tooth was broken, his body was battered, and blood flowed down from where his helmet had pierced his face. Somehow, after bleeding at their hands yet again, the Messenger of Allah ﷺ still had the resilience of character to say as he wiped the blood from his face, 'O Allah, forgive my people, for they do not know.'[51] In other narrations, he first said, 'How can a people succeed after they have wounded their Prophet and soaked him in blood as he calls them to Allah?' Then, he fell silent for a moment, before appealing to Allah with the prayer for forgiveness.

Despite the tragic losses suffered in the Battle of Uḥud, and despite experiencing and witnessing the torture of the Quraysh for years, the Messenger of Allah ﷺ maintained magnanimity. His Companions came to him ﷺ and said as the dust cleared, 'Curse the polytheists.' He said, 'I have not been sent as one who curses. Rather, I was sent as a mercy.'[52] Although the Qur'an mentions that the wicked ones of the

[51] Collected by al-Bukhārī (6530) and Muslim (1792).

[52] Collected by Muslim (2599).

Israelites were cursed on the tongue of their Prophets,[53] and even though the Prophet ﷺ cursed certain actions[54] and initially asked Allah to curse the leading persecutors,[55] his normative mode was to seek forgiveness for those who wronged him and his followers.

53 *'Cursed were those who disbelieved among the Children of Israel by the tongue of David and of Jesus, the son of Mary. That was because they disobeyed and [habitually] transgressed'* (al-Mā'idah 5:78).

54 The Prophet ﷺ said, 'Allah has cursed *ribā* (interest), its consumer, its payer, its [contract] documenter, its witnesses. They are all equal.' Collected by Muslim (1598).

55 The Prophet ﷺ invoked Allah to curse the likes of Ṣafwān ibn Umayyah, Suhayl ibn 'Amr, and al-Ḥārith ibn Hishām, but desisted when Allah ﷻ revealed, *'You do not have any decision in the matter whether He will forgive them or punish them'* (Āl-'Imrān 3:128). Collected by al-Bukhārī (4283), et al.

25 Forgiving Treason

Upon returning from Uḥud, there were many Companions whose emotions were ablaze from the calamity that had just befallen them who called for the execution of ʿAbdullāh ibn Ubayy ibn Salūl. After all, he had deserted them just before the battle, taking a third of the army back with him, saying, 'He obeyed them [who wanted to march out] and disobeyed me [who wanted to fight from within Madinah]. Why should we get ourselves killed?' The Messenger of Allah ﷺ did not have Ibn Salūl executed for this crime of treason lest rumours spread that Muhammad kills his own followers, and in hope that some of the hypocrites might turn over a new leaf.[56]

[56] In *Sharh Muslim* (6/167), Imam an-Nawawī explains that the secret behind the Messenger of Allah ﷺ reciting *Sūrah al-Munāfiqūn* (the Hypocrites) in particular during the Friday prayer is that it prompted them to repent before their window of opportunity closes, as the hypocrites would attend this congregation more than any other.

26 God Informed Him of an Assassination Attempt

While sitting with Ṣafwān ibn Umayyah one night at the Kaʿbah, lamenting the loss of those who had been killed or captured by the Muslims at Badr, ʿUmayr swore that had it not been for his debts and many dependents, he would have rode out to Madinah and assassinated Muhammad ﷺ. Ṣafwān ibn Umayyah vowed to cover his debts and care for his family, and so ʿUmayr traveled to Madinah after sharpening and poisoning his sword. ʿUmar ؓ and the Companions were suspicious of his intentions, but the Prophet ﷺ ordered them to let him enter. When he claimed to be coming for a relative of his among the captives, the Messenger ﷺ admonished him to be honest and noted that the sword he carried told a different tale. ʿUmayr kept to his story, so the Prophet ﷺ informed him of the details of conversation he had secretly had with Ṣafwān and then told him that Allah would prevent him from accomplishing this mission. ʿUmayr then testified that he was the Messenger of Allah, recognizing that nobody could have brought him this news but Allah.[57]

---

[57] Collected by al-Bayhaqī in Dalāʾil an-Nubuwwa (3/147–149), Ibn Saʿd in at-Tabaqāt (4/200) and al-Haythamī in Majmaʿ az-Zawāʾid (8/286) who attributed it to at-Ṭabarānī. The best of these chains of transmission is a sound mursal report traceable to ʿUrwah and another mursal report attributed to Anas ؓ. Thus, researchers have extensively debated these accounts, especially the details about ʿUmayr embracing Islam after Badr.

27 Forgiving a Sorcerer

Labīd ibn al-Aʿsam was a young man who used to serve the Prophet Muhammad ﷺ and was paid by members of his tribe to employ witchcraft against the Messenger of Allah ﷺ. For six months, the Prophet ﷺ was weakened and mentally fatigued by these incantations, though this only affected his worldly engagements. Once Labīd ibn al-Aʿsam was exposed, and permission was sought to execute him, he said, 'No. As for me, Allah has cured me. And I do not wish to stir evil among the people.'[58]

[58] Collected by al-Bukhārī (5765) and Muslim (2189). In *Fatḥ al-Bārī*, Ibn Hajar explains that Labīd sought forgiveness, and pleaded that he only did this out of need for the money, and so the Messenger of Allah ﷺ did not want to stir hostilities between the people, nor for it to be said that Muhammad kills his followers, since Labīd was among those tribes who feigned Islam.

28 A Blessed Woman

After the Battle of Banū al-Muṣṭaliq, Juwayriah bint al-Ḥārith رضي الله عنها, the daughter of Banū al-Muṣṭaliq's chief, was purchased and emancipated from Thābit ibn Qays رضي الله عنه by the Messenger of Allah ﷺ. Then, he married her, and as a result the Muslims freed one hundred men from Banū al-Muṣṭaliq, all of whom accepted Islam. The Companions said, 'These are [now] the in-laws of Allah's Messenger! ﷺ' Clearly, the Prophet ﷺ knew that marrying this noble woman would persuade his Companions to free her people, and Juwayriah رضي الله عنها knew this as well. For that reason, 'Ā'ishah رضي الله عنها used to praise her and say, 'I do not know any woman who was a greater blessing for her people than her.'[59]

59 See: *al-Bidāyah wan-Nihāyah* (4/159).

29 An Attempted Coup

During the campaign of Banū al-Muṣṭaliq, ʿAbdullāh ibn Ubayy had sworn, *'If we return to Madinah, the honourable among us (referring to himself) will expel the humiliated (referring to the Prophet ﷺ)'* (*al-Munāfiqūn* 63:8) News of this reached the Prophet ﷺ, and ʿUmar رضي الله عنه said, 'O Messenger of Allah, allow me to strike the neck of this hypocrite.' He said, 'Leave him. The people must not say Muhammad kills his companions.'[60] In fact, ibn Ubayy's own son heard this insult and came forward and said, 'I have heard that you wish to kill my father due to what has reached you about him [insulting you]. If you are going to do this, then instruct me and I will bring his head to you (for I may not bear seeing my father's killer).' He said, 'Rather, let us be gentle with him, and give him kind companionship for as long as he remains with us.'[61]

---

60 Collected by al-Bukhārī (3518) and Muslim (2584).

61 Collected by Ibn Hishām (2/291).

30 'Let Them Cool Off'

The tribe of Banū Quraydhah had reneged on its pact with the Prophet ﷺ by conspiring to bring the Quraysh and Ghatafān into Madinah to annihilate every trace of the newly budding Muslim community. After the invaders laid a month-long siege to Madinah, wherein the Muslims were trapped and starving in their trenches, Allah destined that the confederates begin suspecting one another and lose their zeal to continue the siege. Despite his fledgling community having just been on the verge of eradication, the Prophet ﷺ did not respond to this betrayal with a desire for vengeance. After the Muslim army raced up to Banū Quraydhah's dwellings, the Messenger of Allah ﷺ not only let this enemy tribe choose their own ally (Saʿd ibn Muʿādh) to determine their penalty, but even said to his Companions upon seeing the captives of Banū Quraydhah waiting in the sun, 'Do not compound for them the Sun's heat atop the heat of their armor. Give them shade and drink, so that they may cool off.'[62]

62 See: *as-Sayr al-Kabīr* (2/591) by ash-Shaybānī.

31 'Ignore Their Insults'

Allah wished to terminate the widespread practice of adopting a child and failing to preserve their lineage. However, this institution was so ingrained in Arabia's culture that challenging it would only be accepted from the Prophet ﷺ himself, as only he was infallible and above criticism. For this reason, Allah instructed His Prophet ﷺ to desist from calling his adopted son Zayd ibn Ḥārithah (formerly Zayd ibn Muhammad) by other than his true paternal name. But to unequivocally establish that an adopted child was to maintain their own lineage, Allah then ordered (also in *Sūrah al-Aḥzāb*) him to marry Zayd's wife once Zayd had divorced her. Of course, the hypocrites pounced on this opportunity to accuse the Prophet ﷺ of being a licentious man who marries his daughter-in-law, and an imposter who forbade people from marrying their sons' wives but accepted it for himself.[63] This was no harmless insult, but yet another attempt to develop a critical mass of Madinans who would overthrow the new head of state. The Prophet ﷺ did not punish them; rather, he ignored them completely and left the matter to God, just as his Lord had instructed him. 'And do not mind the disbelievers and the hypocrites. Ignore their harm and rely upon Allah. And sufficient is Allah as a Disposer of [your] affairs' (*al-Aḥzāb* 33:48) This was a time when the Prophet ﷺ

63 See: *Tafsīr al-Qurṭubī*; [*al-Aḥzāb* (33):37].

was well established, around four to five years after his migration, and could have easily punished those who insulted him. But the Qur'an instructed him to ignore them just as he did in Makkah.

32 'Do You Not Love That Allah Should Forgive You?'

Misṭaḥ was among those who fell into slandering 'Ā'ishah ﵂. Following the return from Banū al-Muṣṭaliq, 'Abdullāh ibn Ubayy began spreading rumours that the Messenger of Allah ﷺ's wife had committed adultery. After a month-long ordeal of suspicions and tensions in the Muslim community, Allah finally revealed verses in *Sūrah an-Nūr* exposing the ringleaders behind this lie, but not before some of the believers had begun to believe and circulate this unfounded story. Misṭaḥ ﵁ was one of those genuine believers who made the mistake of repeating this accusation. Not only did the Prophet ﷺ ultimately forgive this man who had slandered his wife, but he even admonished Abū Bakr ﵁—her father—for boycotting him, especially since he was related to Abū Bakr and used to receive charity from him. 'Ā'ishah ﵂ said:

> Abū Bakr swore that he would never spend on Misṭaḥ again, but then Allah revealed the verse, *'Let not those among you who are virtuous and wealthy swear not to give to their kin and those in need. Do you not love that Allah should forgive you? And Allah is Most Forgiving, Most Merciful'* (*an-Nūr* 24:22). On hearing that, Abū Bakr ﵁ said, 'Yes, by Allah, O our Lord! We wish that You should forgive us.' And Abū Bakr resumed his stipend.[64]

[64] Collected by al-Bukhārī (60/281).

33 Raided in Ḥudaybiyyah Valley

After the Prophet ﷺ and 1,400 of his Companions arrived in their austere ritual garb at the outskirts of Makkah, seeking only to perform *'umrah*, news spread in Makkah that the Muslims had come to vanquish them. Anas ibn Mālik ؓ said:

> Eighty men swooped down from Makkah upon the Messenger of Allah ﷺ from the mountain of Tan'īm. They were armed and seeking to attack the Prophet ﷺ and his Companions by surprise. However, he captured them and spared their lives [freeing them without ransom], and about this Allah revealed, *'And it is He who withheld their hands from you and your hands from them within [the area of] Makkah after He caused you to overcome them.'* (*al-Fatḥ* 48:24)

Allah establishes that He conferred two great favours upon the Muslims in this incident. The first was that they became aware of the attack before it caught them off guard, and the second was that He inspired the Prophet ﷺ to forgive and release the prisoners.[65]

[65] See: *Tafsīr Ibn "Āshūr; (al-Fatḥ* 48:24].

34 Hosting the Insulting Ambassador

ʿUrwah ibn Masʿūd ﵁, while still a pagan, participated on behalf of the Quraysh in what became the Treaty of Ḥudaybiyyah. Amidst the negotiations, he behaved condescendingly towards the Messenger of Allah ﷺ by reaching out to pull his beard, despite the Companions threatening him with their weapons. He also insulted the Prophet ﷺ by saying that he was no match for the Quraysh, 'And I do not think you will be able [to defeat them]. And if war does erupt, by Allah, I do not see around you except an undignified bunch that would quickly flee and desert you.' Despite such insolence, and the fact that ʿUrwah ibn Masʿūd was a chief from the tribe of Thaqīf—who had assaulted him ﷺ in Ṭā'if—he honoured this ambassador's stay and hosted him for as long as he wished.[66]

[66] Collected by al-Bukhārī (2731, 2732) and Muslim (4401–4409).

35 Eager for Peace

Suhayl ibn ʿAmr ﵁ was sent next by the Quraysh to finalize the Treaty of Ḥudaybiyyah. Even before demanding oppressive double standards in the treaty, Suhayl ibn ʿAmr forcefully objected to it being documented as an agreement between the Quraysh and the Messenger of Allah ﷺ. He said, 'If we believed you were the Messenger of God, we would not have fought you' and insisted that the title Messenger of Allah be erased. ʿAlī ibn Abī Ṭālib ﵁ refused to erase it, but the Prophet ﷺ obliged, not allowing his personal pride to deter him from making peace with the Quraysh as he was intent on avoiding bloodshed in the sacred sanctuary of Makkah. For that same reason, he reluctantly accepted to send back Abū Jandal ﵁, the son and escaped prisoner of Suhyal ibn ʿAmr, to Makkah for the greater good.

This was pure mercy and piety, not timidity, because the Prophet ﷺ had initially said to Budayl ibn Warqāʾ, the Quraysh's first ambassador to the Muslims at al-Ḥudaybiyyah, 'We did not come to fight. We came for *ʿumrah*, although we know that the Quraysh is worn out from warfare.'[67] Imam az-Zuhrī, a sub-narrator of this hadith, said, 'He did this because he declared [upon reaching al-Ḥudaybiyyah], "They will not offer me any proposition which glorifies the sanctities of Allah except that I will accept it from them."'

[67] Collected by al-Bukhārī (2731, 2732) and Muslim (4401–4409).

36 'These Are Your Rights'

When Thaqīf kidnapped two Muslims shortly before Khaybar, the Prophet ﷺ was able to capture a man from Banū 'Uqayl, an ally of Thaqīf, in order to exchange him for the Muslim prisoners. This man kept calling out, 'O Muhammad, on what basis did you apprehend me?...O Muhammad, I am a Muslim... O Muhammad, I am hungry so give me food, and I am thirsty so bring me drink.' Despite him repeatedly calling the head of state by his first name, and despite him pestering the Prophet ﷺ every time he left, the Messenger of Allah ﷺ answered his questions with incredible humility, and responded to his requests by saying, 'These are your rights.'[68] Thus was the ocean of his compassion, his respect for the humanity of his enemies, and how he empathized with their distress.

68 Collected by Muslim (1641), Abū Dāwūd (3316), Ibn Ḥibbān (4859), ash-Shāfiʿi (1490), ad-Dāraqutnī (37), al-Bayhaqī in *as-Sunan al-Kubrā* (1845), and Abū Nuʿaym in *Ḥilyat al-Awliyāʾ* (8/651).

37 The Mother of His Companion

Abū Hurayrah's mother appears to have migrated to Madinah with her son without having accepted Islam, because Abū Hurayrah ﷺ said:

> I used to invite my mother to Islam while she was still a polytheist. One day, when I invited her, she said words I could not bear to hear about the Messenger of Allah ﷺ. I went to the Messenger of Allah ﷺ weeping, and said, 'O Messenger of Allah, I invite my mother to Islam and she [always] refuses me. Today, when I invited her, she said words about you that I could not bear to hear, so invoke Allah that He guide the mother of Abū Hurayrah.' The Messenger of Allah ﷺ said, 'O Allah, guide the mother of Abū Hurayrah!' I walked out, optimistic due to the Prophet's supplication. When I came [home] and reached the door, I found it locked. My mother heard the sound of my feet. She said, 'Stay where you are, O Abū Hurayrah', and I could hear water running. She bathed herself, wore her garments, and quickly donned her headgear. She then opened the door, and said following that, 'O Abū Hurayrah, I testify that none is worthy of worship except Allah, and I testify that Muhammad is His slave and Messenger.' I went back to the Messenger ﷺ crying from joy. I said [to him], 'O Messenger of Allah, rejoice! Allah has responded to your supplication and guided the mother of Abū Hurayrah.'

He ﷺ praised Allah, exalted Him, and said good words. I said, 'O Messenger of Allah, invoke Allah to make me and my mother beloved to His believing slaves, and to make them beloved to us.' The Messenger of Allah ﷺ said, 'O Allah, make this small slave of Yours and his mother beloved to Your believing slaves, and make the believers beloved to them.' Thereafter, no believer has existed that hears of me, and does not [even] see me, except that he loves me.'[69]

It should be noted that the Prophet ﷺ was aware of the insults of Abū Hurayrah's mother, but did not take any action against her. Instead, he supplicated for her. This incident, due to the late arrival of Abū Hurayrah رضي الله عنه in Madinah, took place in the last three years of the Prophet's ﷺ life when he had undeniable authority over the citizens of Madinah.

[69] Collected by Muslim (2491).

38 'Who Will Protect You from Me?'

On their return from the Battle of Dhāt ar-Riqāʿ, which occurred in the 7th *hijri* year, the Messenger of Allah ﷺ and his Companions dismounted and dispersed in a valley seeking shade from the midday Sun. The Messenger of Allah ﷺ camped under a leafy tree and hung his sword on it. The army slept for a while, but then heard the Messenger of Allah ﷺ calling for them. Jābir ibn ʿAbdillāh says:

> We came to him, and sitting with him was a Bedouin man (al-Ḥākim adds: named al-Ghawrath ibn al-Ḥārith). The Messenger of Allah ﷺ said, 'This person drew my sword as I slept, and I awoke to find an unsheathed blade in his hand.' He said to me, 'Are you afraid of me?' I said, 'No.' He said, 'Who will protect you from me?' I said, 'Allah' thrice, and so he returned the sword to its scabbard. And thus, here he is, sitting.[70]

Jābir added, 'And the Messenger of Allah ﷺ did not punish him thereafter.'[71] In another narration, the sword fell from his hand, so the Messenger of Allah ﷺ took it and said:

[70] In *Fatḥ al-Bārī* (7/426), Ibn Ḥajar said, 'When the Bedouin witnessed this great firmness, and recognized that something had come between him [and the Prophet ﷺ], it is as if he verified his truthfulness and became certain that he would not reach him. This is why he threw down the weapon and lowered his guard.'

[71] Collected by al-Bukhārī (2910) and Muslim (843).

> Who will protect you [from me]? He said, 'Be the better [victor].' He said, 'Will you [now] testify that none is worthy of worship except Allah?' He said, 'I will promise to never fight you, nor be with a people that fight you.' At that, the Messenger of Allah ﷺ let him go, and so the man went to his people and said, 'I have come to you from the best of people.'[72]

The implication is that the Prophet ﷺ forgave him and let him go and did not force him to convert.

[72] Collected by al-Ḥākim (4322) who graded it authentic according to the criteria of al-Bukhārī and Muslim. Imam adh-Dhahabī agreed with him, and al-Albāni authenticated it in at-Taʿlīqāt al-Hisān (2872).

39 A Powerful Prisoner

Thumāmah ibn Uthāl ﵁ was the chief of Banū Ḥanīfah who had assassinated a number of the Prophet's Companions, and had even plotted to kill the Prophet ﷺ himself. Though he had permitted killing Thumāmah in light of his murderous record, his treatment of Thumāmah as a captive was a clear indication that the Messenger of Allah ﷺ remained hopeful that he would become Muslim and earn the forgiveness of Allah. After being caught and fastened to a column in the Prophet's ﷺ mosque, Thumāmah received the utmost kindness and hospitality from the Messenger ﷺ—to the degree that milk from the Prophet's ﷺ personal she-camel would be carried to his place of bondage. Each day, the Prophet ﷺ would patiently ask Thumāmah to consider Islam, before finally ordering his Companions to release this man. But when that happened, Thumāmah went to a garden of date-palm trees near the mosque, took a bath and then entered the mosque and said:

> I testify that none has the right to be worshipped except Allah, and testify that Muhammad is His Messenger! O Muhammad, I swear by Allah that there was no face on the surface of the earth more disliked by me than yours, but now your face has become the most beloved face to me.

By Allah, there was no religion more disliked by me than yours, but now it is the most beloved religion to me. By Allah, there was no town more disliked by me than your town, but now it is the most beloved town to me.[73]

[73] Collected by al-Bukhārī (4372) and Muslim (1764).

40 Sparing the Quraysh Again

Once Thumāmah embraced Islam, he journeyed back to his people, the tribe of al-Yamāmah, and they soon followed him in entering the fold of Islam. Upon doing so, they boycotted the Quraysh and refused to send any more grain—which the Quraysh heavily depended on—their way. Such a sanction would have been highly effective in draining whatever strength the Quraysh had left, but the Messenger ﷺ interceded on their behalf, despite being at war with them, because of his concern for the innocent people behind enemy lines. Responding to the Prophet's ﷺ instructions, the tribe of al-Yamāmah resumed its ordinary trade with Makkah, saving the city that had itself boycotted the Prophet ﷺ for so many years.[74]

[74] See: *as-Sīrah* (4/284–285) by Ibn Hishām.

41 'Did You Check His Heart?'

In Ramadan of the 7th *hijri* year, the Prophet ﷺ sent a battalion of his Companions to fight the People of Ghālib, and regarding that battle Usāmah ibn Zayd ؓ gave the following account:

> An Anṣārī man and I pursued one of their men. Once we were upon him, he said, 'There is no God but Allah (*Lā ilāha illā Allāh).*' On hearing that, the Anṣārī man pulled back, but I killed him by stabbing him with my spear. When we returned [to Madinah], the Prophet ﷺ came to know about the incident and said, 'O Usāmah! Did you kill him after he said '*lā ilāha illā Allāh*?' I said, 'But he [only] said this to save himself.' The Prophet ﷺ said, 'O Usāmah! Did you kill him after he said '*Lā ilāha illā Allāh*?' And he kept repeating this until I wished I had not embraced Islam before that day![75]

In the narration of al-Aʿmash, the Prophet ﷺ rebuked Usāmah by saying, 'Did you check his heart?' It made no difference that this man presumably became Muslim to save his skin.

[75] Collected by al-Bukhārī (83/11) and Muslim (1/176-178).

It made no difference that this was none other than Usāmah ibn Zayd رضي الله عنه, the son of Zayd ibn Ḥārithah رضي الله عنه, and hence as dear to the Prophet ﷺ as his own grandchildren. None of that mattered because this was the Messenger of Allah ﷺ—incredibly charitable in his judgment of others' sincerity.

42 The Sword of Allah

This was the nickname of Khālid ibn Walīd ﵁, the military genius who led the charge from behind at Uḥud and massacred many Muslims. But after four years of watching the Muslims' resilience on the battlefield, he became increasingly convinced that unseen forces were, in fact, supporting them. In the seventh year (*hijri*), the Prophet ﷺ married Maymunah bint al-Ḥārith ﵁, Khālid's maternal aunt, after completing his *'umrah* in Makkah, and sent a letter to Khālid inviting him to Islam.

This could have been a trap, a ploy to assassinate the Quraysh's most accomplished general, but Khālid dismissed that notion as he knew that Muhammad's ﷺ integrity was virtually undisputed. When Khālid travelled to Madinah a few months later to embrace Islam, the Prophet ﷺ received him with a 'beaming smile' and said, 'All praise be to Allah who guided you. I had long seen you as having a piercing intellect that made me hopeful that it would only lead you to good.' He said, 'O Messenger of Allah, you saw how many battles I participated in against you, stubbornly defying the truth. Supplicate to Allah that He may forgive me for these [crimes].' He replied, 'O Allah, forgive Khālid for all he did in deterring [others] from Your path.'[76]

76 Collected by al-Wāqidī (2/749).

43 Islam Does Away With the Past

'Amr ibn al-'Āṣ ﷺ was another military commander who had long fought against Islam, and he made the journey with Khālid ibn al-Walīd ﷺ to the Messenger of Allah ﷺ in Madinah. Ibn Shumāsah al-Mahrī reports that when he visited 'Amr ibn al-'Ās ﷺ, as he was on his deathbed:

> 'Amr turned his face towards the wall and wept for a long time. His son said, 'O father! Did not the Messenger of Allah ﷺ give you the glad tidings of such and such?' He turned his face [towards them] and said, 'The best thing we can rely on is the testimony that none is worthy of worship except Allah and that Muhammad ﷺ is the Messenger of Allah. Indeed, I have passed through three phases [in my life]. I [first] found myself loathing no one more than I loathed the Messenger of Allah ﷺ and there was no desire stronger in me than that I should vanquish him and kill him. Had I died in this state, I would have definitely been one of the residents of the Fire.
>
> When Allah instilled the love of Islam in my heart, I came to the Prophet ﷺ and said, 'Stretch out your right hand so that I may pledge allegiance to you.' But when he outstretched his right hand, I withdrew my hand.

The Prophet ﷺ said, 'What happened, O 'Amr?' I replied, 'I wish to lay down some conditions.' He asked, 'What conditions do you want to put forward?' I said, 'That I should be granted pardon.' He said, "Don't you know that Islam wipes out everything before it, and that migration wipes out everything before it, and that Hajj wipes out everything before it?" Thereafter, no one was dearer to me than the Messenger of Allah ﷺ, and none was more exalted in my eyes than him. I could not even stare at him directly out of reverence for him, and thus if I am asked to describe his features, I would not [be able to] describe them, for I have never eyed him fully.[77]

77 Collected by Muslim (711).

44 Allah Loves Those Who Act Justly

During the truce effected by the Treaty of al-Ḥudaybiyyah, Qutaylah bint ʿAbdil ʿUzzā visited her daughter, Asmāʾ bint Abī Bakr , in Madinah. Asmāʾ says, 'My mother came to me, hopeful [for financial support] during the time of the Prophet , so I asked the Prophet , "Should I uphold ties with her?" He said, 'Yes."'[78]

Though this may seem unremarkable, the Prophet was allowing a pagan woman, from an enemy tribe, to stay in the home of two high-profile men of state, for Asmāʾ was the daughter of Abū Bakr as-Ṣiddīq and the wife of az-Zubayr ibn al-ʿAwwām . This may have been why she hesitated about admitting her mother into the home, lest her mother assassinate either of these personalities or gather some sensitive information. Ibn ʿUyaynah, a sub-narrator of this hadith, said that it was regarding her that Allah revealed, *'Allah does not forbid you regarding those who do not fight you because of religion and do not expel you from your homes from being righteous toward them and acting justly toward them. Indeed, Allah loves those who act justly' (al-Mumtaḥanah 60:8).*

---

78 Collected by al-Bukhārī (801) and Muslim (2194).

Marching to Makkah: A Conquest Like No Other

Before diving into the Conquest of Makkah, and in order to fathom its epic nature, one must first put oneself in the Prophet's place ﷺ. He is marching amidst 10,000 strong, heading in full force to oust the Quraysh from the sacred precincts. These were the same Quraysh who had persecuted him in every way imaginable for thirteen years in Makkah. These were the same Quraysh who had executed his Companions, caused the death of his wife, Khadījah, assaulted his children, expelled him from his homeland, injured him at Uḥud, mobilized to annihilate his nation at al-Aḥzāb, and signed a treaty (al-Ḥudaybiyyah) that they quickly broke. Now, after over 20 years of relentless hostilities, the Prophet Muhammad ﷺ catches the Makkans off guard, standing before him completely powerless with no possibility of resistance.

45 Abū Jahl's Partner

When the Prophet ﷺ entered upon his dying uncle, Abū Ṭālib, ʿAbdullāh ibn Abī Umayyah was there along with Abū Jahl. Despite the Prophet Muhammad's ﷺ desperate pleas to Abū Ṭālib, ʿAbdullāh ibn Abī Umayyah shamed the Prophet's uncle from embracing Islam before his final breath.[79] This became known as the most difficult year in the Prophet's life ﷺ: The Year of Grief. The grief was not due to only losing his dear uncle, his longest caregiver, and his strongest supporter; it was compounded by the knowledge that a reunion with Abū Ṭālib in the afterlife was impossible. A decade later, just prior to the Muslims marching into Makkah, ʿAbdullāh ibn Abī Umayyah approached the Muslim camp intending to accept Islam at the hands of its Prophet. However, the Prophet ﷺ kept refusing to allow him to enter. With the help of his half-sister, Umm Salamah رضي الله عنها, who was the Prophet's ﷺ wife, he continued to ask for clemency from the Prophet ﷺ, reminding him that he was family (a brother-in-law), and that he had forgiven people who had committed greater crimes than him. The Prophet ﷺ ultimately said to him what Joseph عليه السلام said to his brothers who had carved similar scars in him by separating him from his father: *'No blame will there be on you today'* (*Yūsuf* 12:92).[80]

[79] Collected by al-Bukhārī (1360) in Kitāb al-Janā'iz.

[80] See: *al-Isābah fī taʿrīf as-Ṣaḥābah* (4/12).

46 'Whoever Enters the Home of Abū Sufyān'

Abū Sufyān ibn Ḥarb was no ordinary enemy or warmonger. He had been the staunchest enemy of the Prophet for two decades. He was also among those who convened in Dār an-Nadwah to plan the assassination of Prophet Muhammad ﷺ before he migrated to Madinah. Since Badr, he had sworn to lead the fight against the Messenger of Allah ﷺ, and he even raided Madinah one night and killed two Anṣārī men before fleeing.[81] After leading the pagans at Uḥud, he said to the Muslims, 'Among the dead, you will find bodies that were mutilated. I neither ordered this, nor does it bother me!'[82] Both this incident, and his laying siege to Madinah (seeking to murder even the women and children), were not known practices among the Arabs, which reflects his bloodlust for Muslims. Given all these details and more, how did the Messenger of Allah ﷺ treat him when the tide turned? Upon discovering that the Muslim army had just taken them by surprise, Abū Sufyān found himself paralyzed and unable to think. He knew with absolute certainty that he was atop the most wanted list. However, al-'Abbās ؓ interceded for him, and he embraced Islam the next day along with 'Abdullāh ibn Abī Umayyah. The Prophet ﷺ forgave everything, granted him security, and even promised him

[81] See: *al-Bidāyah wan-Nihāyah* (2/540).

[82] Collected by al-Bukhārī (3817), Abū Dāwūd (2262), and an-Nasā'ī (8635).

that any Makkan who entered his home would be safe![83] The fact that even this man's feelings—a man who caused so much pain to the Prophet ﷺ—were taken into consideration indicates the extraordinary nature of his heart.

83 Dr. Ragheb Sergani comments, 'Look at this virtue, this greatness! A person cannot wrap his head around what just happened until he puts himself in this situation. Let us be honest with ourselves, and the world with itself; would anyone ever do this but the Messenger of Allah ﷺ? Are there still people claiming that Muslims do not acknowledge "the other", and do not understand coexistence? Is Islam still the religion of terror and savagery in people's minds? Our real crisis is knowledge; once someone bypasses the superficial acquaintance with Allah's Messenger ﷺ—he/she realizes how empty theory is in the presence of facts.' Adapted from 'The Prophet's Tolerance with His Enemies', an article on www.islamstory.com.

47 'Today is the Day of Mercy'

Abū Sufyān ﷺ, now a Muslim, rides ahead to Makkah and encourages his people to surrender, reassuring them that whoever enters his house will not be harmed. The Muslims ride into Makkah, led by the Prophet ﷺ, who kept his head lowered out of humility for Allah to the point that his beard almost touched his saddle.[84] It reached him ﷺ that some were saying, 'O Abū Sufyān, today is the day of [your people's] slaughter. Today, the Kaʿbah is not a sanctuary.' In response, he announced, 'Rather, this is the day in which Allah will glorify the Kaʿbah, and the day when the Kaʿbah will be garbed.'[85]

In another narration: 'Today is the day of mercy. Today Allah will honour the Quraysh.'[86]

After securing the city, everyone gathered before the Prophet ﷺ at the Kaʿbah, and he asked them tenderly, 'O gathering of the Quraysh, what do you think I will do to you?' They said, 'Only good, [O] noble brother, son of

84 See: *as-Sīrah* (4/1072) by Ibn Hishām.

85 Collected by al-Bukhārī (40300 and al-Bayhaqī in as-Sunan al-Kubrā (18058).

86 See: *Fatḥ al-Bārī* (8/9).

> a noble brother.' Ending the moment of suspense, he declared, 'I will only say to you what Joseph said to his brothers, *"No blame will there be upon you today"* (*Yūsuf* 12:92). Go, for you are unbound.'[87]

The Prophet ﷺ rose above it all, immortalizing himself with this grace in one of the most remarkable events in human history.

Even the Anṣār marvelled at this profound benevolence to the point that some said, 'This man has been overcome by his hopefulness for [returning to] his town, and by compassion for his kin.' Abū Hurayrah رضي الله عنه said:

> And then revelation came, and when he ﷺ was receiving revelation, it was not hidden from us. When it came, none of us would dare raise our eyes to the Messenger of Allah ﷺ until the revelation finished. When the revelation concluded, the Messenger of Allah ﷺ said, 'O gathering of Anṣār!' They said, 'At your service, O Messenger of Allah.' He said, 'You have said that this man has been overcome by his hopefulness for his town?' They said, 'Yes, this took place.' He said, 'Never! I am the slave of Allah, and I am His Messenger; I migrated to Allah and towards you. [My] living is with you and [my] dying is with you.' They (the Anṣār) turned towards him in tears, and said, 'By Allah, we only said what we said because of how protective we are of Allah and His Messenger.'

[87] See: *as-Sīrah* (2/411) by Ibn Hishām, *Zād al-Mi'ād* (3/356) by Ibn al-Qayyim, *ar-Rawḍ al-'Unf* (4/170) by as-Suhayli, and *as-Sīrah* (3/570), and *Fatḥ al-Bārī* (8/18) by Ibn Hajar.

> The Messenger of Allah ﷺ said, 'Indeed, Allah and His Messenger believe you, and excuse you.'[88]

What had just happened with the Quraysh was beyond comprehension, even for the Anṣār's beautiful hearts. He understood that comprehending this action of complete forgiveness was difficult, and thus he said, 'and excuse you'.

---

88 Collected by Muslim (4395).

48 Access Granted

ʿUthmān ibn Ṭalḥah رضي الله عنه used to deny the Prophet ﷺ entrance to the Kaʿbah, as he was from Banū ʿAbd ad-Dār, a clan of the Quraysh who took great pride in being the custodians of the key to the Kaʿbah. He would mock the Prophet Muhammad ﷺ and campaign to exterminate the message of Islam. With certitude in the promise of Allah, he ﷺ would simply tell ʿUthmān ibn Ṭalḥah that this key would one day be in his hands. Ibn Jurayj reports that at the Conquest of Makkah, the Prophet ﷺ took the key from ʿUthmān ibn Ṭalḥah. He ﷺ entered the Kaʿbah, then exited while reciting, *'Indeed, Allah instructs you to return the trusts to their rightful owners'* (*an-Nisāʾ* 4:58). Despite his abusive past, the Messenger ﷺ called for ʿUthmān ibn Ṭalḥah, and showed exemplary forgiveness by returning the key to him.[89]

[89] See: *Tafsīr at-Ṭabarī* (8/491–492) and *Tafsīr Ibn Kathīr* (2/340).

49 A Changed Man

Suhayl ibn 'Amr ☝ was now a broken elderly man with a dark history, forced by his failure at extinguishing Islam to request from his son, 'Abdullāh—one of his many children who were now part of the triumphant Muslim army—to plead for asylum on his behalf during the Conquest of Makkah. Without hesitation, the Prophet ﷺ granted him security and went further to say that a man with such honour and intellect should not be oblivious of Islam's merit [for long]. Indeed, Suhayl soon came forward and embraced Islam, and became known for his dedication to ritual worship. In fact, when news of the Prophet ﷺ dying reached Makkah, this man who had long preached against Islam declared, 'O people of Quraysh! Do not be the last to enter Islam and the first to apostate! This religion will extend everywhere that the sun and moon extend to, from the place they rise to the place they set.'[90] This is how the beautiful treatment of the Messenger ﷺ transformed people in unimaginable ways. His fine character, great tolerance, and ability to forget hard feelings, forever shames how victors before and after him enter a city, hunt down its leadership, and exact their revenge merely out of hate, the desire to subjugate, and personal vendetta.

---

[90] See: *Asad al-Ghābah* by Ibn Atheer, *al-Isābah* by Ibn Hajar, and *Fatḥ al-Bārī* also by Ibn Hajar.

50 A Proud Heart Humbled

Ṣafwān ibn Umayyah ﵁ was a vicious antagonist of Islam from its advent. He helped his father, Umayyah ibn Khalaf, torture Bilāl ibn Rabāḥ ﵁, participated in every battle between the Quraysh and the Muslims, sent ʿUmayr ibn Wahb to assassinate the Prophet ﷺ, and supplied Banū Bakr with the weaponry to attack Banū Khuzāʿah (an ally of the Muslims), thereby nullifying the Treaty of Ḥudaybiyyah. Therefore, it would be correct to say that Ṣafwān was a primary reason behind the Prophet's ﷺ decision to march into Makkah, and thus he fled Makkah at its conquest after briefly fighting, unlike the overwhelming majority who peacefully surrendered. He felt dejected and displaced, so ʿUmayr ibn Wahb—now a Muslim—asked the Prophet ﷺ to pardon Safwān's crimes and permit his return. Not only did he agree, but he even gave ʿUmayr his turban as a token of guarantee that he personally promised this protection. When Ṣafwān came forward, the Prophet ﷺ graciously gave him another four months to deliberate before accepting Islam, and showered him with heaps of gifts during this period to warm his heart towards the religion. In the end, his proud heart melted from all this generosity, he accepted Islam, and said, 'By God, the Prophet ﷺ gave me gifts at a point when he was the most hated of people to me. But he kept on giving to me until he became the most beloved of people to me.'[91]

[91] Collected by Muslim (2313)

51 The One Who Mutilated His Uncle

Hind bint 'Utbah was the wife of Abū Sufyān and the daughter of 'Utbah ibn Rabī'ah, two nobles from the Quraysh who were both staunch enemies of the Prophet Muhammad ﷺ. Hind also boiled with venomous hate and personally campaigned against Islam and the Muslims. She was among those who essentially hired Waḥshī to kill Ḥamzah ibn 'Abdul Muṭṭalib ﷺ, the paternal uncle of the Prophet ﷺ, promising him great rewards for avenging her father who was slain at Badr. Many early chroniclers report that she had Ḥamzah's ears and nose cut off and used for a necklace, and some hold that she gouged out his liver and attempted to eat it. When the Prophet ﷺ located his uncle's mutilated body after Uḥud, he wept like never before and bade farewell to his beloved uncle by saying, 'May Allah have mercy on you, my uncle. Indeed, you maintained the ties of kinship, and always rushed to do good.' Five years later, Hind stood at the Conquest of Makkah, protesting against the Quraysh for surrendering to the Muslims. She soon realized that resisting was futile, and that the heavens really did support Muhammad ﷺ, and so she went with other women to him ﷺ and took the pledge of allegiance while veiled. When she announced her identity, the Prophet ﷺ kindly replied, 'Welcome, O Hind.' Touched by the magnanimity of the Messenger ﷺ, she proclaimed, 'By Allah, there was no household that I wished to destroy more than yours, but now there is no household that I wish to honour more than yours.'[92]

[92] Collected by al-Bukhārī (6150, 6628) and Muslim (3234)

52 The Assassin

Waḥshī ibn Ḥarb was an Ethiopian slave belonging to Jubayr ibn Muṭʿim. Due to being an acclaimed spear-thrower, he was promised his freedom in exchange for killing Ḥamzah ibn ʿAbdul Muṭṭalib ﷺ at Uḥud. Waḥshī succeeded in doing so, pleasing the vengeful from the Quraysh whose relatives had been killed by Ḥamzah at Badr and devastating the Prophet ﷺ. Ibn Masʿūd ﷺ says, 'Never did we see the Messenger of Allah ﷺ weep as intensely as he wept for Ḥamzah.'[93]

At the Conquest of Makkah, Waḥshī fled, knowing full well that killing a ruler's family member warranted his death. However, the Prophet ﷺ was unlike any ruler. Waḥshī said, 'I heard that no matter how grave a person's crime against him, the Prophet Muhammad ﷺ always chose forgiveness.' This encouraged him to eventually return to Makkah, embrace Islam, and experience first-hand how the Messenger of Allah ﷺ forgave his enemies.[94] Waḥshī could hardly believe he lived to see this day; he would always remember it and say, 'Allah honoured Ḥamzah ibn ʿAbdulMuṭṭalib and at-Ṭufayl ibn an-Nuʿmān [with martyrdom] at my hand, and did not humiliate me at their hands [by dying upon disbelief].'[95]

---

93 See: *as-Sīrah al-Ḥalabiyyah* (1/461).

94 Collected by al-Bukhārī (3844, 4072), Ahmad (16077), and al-Bayhaqī in *Dalā'il an-Nubuwwa* (3/241).

95 See: *at-Tabaqāt* (3/573) by Ibn Sa'd.

53 A Promise of Security

ʿAbdullāh ibn Saʿd (also known as Ibn Abī as-Sarḥ) was one of the very few whose blood was deemed violable at the Conquest of Makkah. This was because he was guilty of trying to forge records of the Qur'an—after becoming a scribe of revelation. He had fled Madinah, renouncing his Islam, and spreading rumours that 'Muhammad has no idea what he is saying'. At the Conquest of Makkah, he snuck into the house of ʿUthmān ﷺ and pleaded with him to intercede on his behalf with the Prophet ﷺ. ʿUthmān tried numerous times to evoke the Prophet's ﷺ pity for ʿAbdullāh ibn Saʿd, or to simply do a favour to ʿUthmān (who breastfed from this man's mother as a child), before he finally relented. Later, when the Prophet ﷺ asked the Companions why they did not kill this man, they suggested that he should have winked at them. He said, 'It is unbefitting for a Prophet to be someone who employs the treachery of the eye.'

Thereafter, every time ʿAbdullāh ibn Saʿd saw the Messenger of Allah ﷺ, he would run from him. ʿUthmān went to him and said, 'O Messenger of Allah, may my parents be ransomed for you. If only you would see how Ibn Abī as-Sarḥ runs from you whenever he catches sight of you.' The Prophet ﷺ smiled and said, 'Did I not take his pledge and promise him security?'

I said, 'Yes, O Messenger of Allah, but he remembers the gravity of his crime in Islam.' The Prophet ﷺ responded, 'erases whatever is before it.' 'Uthmān ﷺ went back and informed 'Abdullāh ibn Sa'd of this, and he would come and greet the Messenger of Allah ﷺ amidst the people after that. He excelled in his Islam and never turned back again.[96]

96 Collected by Abū Dāwūd (4359) and Ibn Sa'd in *at-Tabaqāt* (339–448).

54 Curing the Heart of a Racist

Abū Maḥdhūrah was a young Pagan who could not bear to see a black man ascend the Kaʿbah and perform the call to prayer (*adhān*) from its roof at the Conquest of Makkah. He and his friends began mocking Bilāl ؓ and imitating his *adhān* with their own voices. The Prophet ﷺ heard his exceptionally beautiful voice and called for him. Abū Maḥdhūrah was brought, likely thinking that he would be executed for mocking Islam. But instead, the Prophet ﷺ wiped his blessed hands over the chest and head of this young man. Abū Maḥdhūrah said, 'By Allah, my heart then filled with belief and conviction that he was the Messenger of Allah.' He embraced Islam, was taught the words of the *adhān*, and was appointed the muezzin of Makkah when the Companions returned to Madinah.[97] Some chroniclers mention that the honorary task of calling *adhān* at the Kaʿbah remained with Abū Maḥdhūrah, and then was inherited by his descendants, for many generations after his death.

97 See: *ar-Rawḍ al-ʿUnf* (7/239).

55 The Touch of Compassion

After the Conquest of Makkah, there were some whose hearts were not won over easily. Faḍālah ibn ʿUmayr was one of those seething with hatred and desperate for revenge. He vowed to kill the Prophet Muhammad ﷺ, despite proclaiming to have accepted Islam. One day, as the Prophet ﷺ was circling the Kaʿbah, Faḍālah tucked his sword under his clothing and followed him closely, gradually coming within attacking range, thinking about the dastardly deed he was about to commit. Suddenly, the Prophet ﷺ turned around and found himself face to face with Faḍālah. 'What was it that you were saying to yourself?' the Prophet asked. 'Nothing. I was just praising Allah' Faḍālah said. The Prophet ﷺ simply smiled and said, 'Ask Allah to forgive you', placing his hand on Faḍālah's chest, transmitting tranquility to him. Faḍālah would say, 'By Allah, from the moment he ﷺ lifted his hand from my chest, there remained nothing of Allah's creation except that he was more beloved to me than it.'[98] This is an assassin in the most sacred place, fully under the Prophet's control, being met with the loving supplication of the Prophet ﷺ rather than the punishment he deserved.

98 See: *ar-Rawḍ al-ʿUnf* (7/114).

56 His Daughter's Persecutor

Habbār ibn Al-Aswad had inflicted the Prophet Muhammad ﷺ with a very personal wound. When his daughter, Zaynab ؓ, tried to migrate from Makkah to Madinah, Habbār caught up with her and continued poking her camel with a spear until it threw her to the ground. Zaynab ؓ suffered a miscarriage from this fall in addition to serious injuries that severely affected her health and contributed to her death several years later. It was an excruciating blow for the Prophet ﷺ to lose his first unborn grandchild and then also his dear daughter. Despite that, when Habbār came begging for exoneration at the Conquest of Makkah, the Prophet of Mercy ﷺ forgave him despite having the means and justification to exact the revenge he merited.[99]

99 Collected by al-Ḥākim (2812), and see: *Fatḥ al-Bārī* (8/11).

57 The Son of Abū Lahab

ʿUtbah and his brother, ʿUtaybah, were two sons of Abū Lahab who he had forced to divorce the Prophet's ﷺ daughters, out of hatred for Muhammad and his new religion. At the Conquest of Makkah, the Prophet ﷺ asked al-ʿAbbās about ʿUtbah and another brother of his, Miʿtab. After being told they had fled Makkah, he ﷺ had al-ʿAbbās chase after them and bring them home. Al-ʿAbbās found his nephews at ʿArafah, and brought them to the Messenger of Allah ﷺ, who invited them to Islam. They accepted, and ʿUtbah displayed great valour by the Prophet's ﷺ side at Ḥunayn and at-Ṭā'if, surely feeling captivated by the grace of a man he had tried to dishonour twenty years earlier.

58 The Son of Abū Jahl

‘Ikrimah ibn Abī Jahl ؓ was not just an enemy because his father (Abū Jahl) was the pharaoh of this nation. He was titled The Lion of the Quraysh for his ferocity, led the Quraysh's left flank against the Muslims at Uḥud as well as an attack against the Muslims at al-Aḥzāb, and was one of the few who took up arms at the Conquest of Makkah and fought the Muslims before giving up and fleeing. After a near-death experience at sea, ‘Ikrimah kept the vow he made to Allah for saving him by returning to seek Muhammad's ﷺ forgiveness. His wife, Umm Ḥakīm, now a Muslim, helped persuade him to keep his vow, and obtained for him a promise of security from the Prophet ﷺ. Upon reaching Makkah, news spread that 'the son of the enemy of Allah' is coming, to which the Prophet ﷺ remarkably responded, 'Indeed, ‘Ikrimah is coming your way as a faithful migrant, so be sure not to insult his father, for insulting the dead grieves the living and does not reach the dead.' When ‘Ikrimah finally arrived, the Prophet ﷺ leapt up to receive him, welcoming his former persecutor with genuine affection.[100] ‘Ikrimah subsequently became one of the most passionate defenders of Islam until he was martyred at the Battle of Yarmūk.

---

[100] Collected by al-Ḥakim (5103).

59 A Change of Tune

Kaʿb ibn Zuhayr ﵁ was a famous Arab poet who had written satirical verses about the Prophet Muhammad ﷺ. In Arabia, such poetry was not only an attack on the core of Islam, but a choice political weapon as well; poets served as propagandists in times of conflict. The Prophet ﷺ had ordered the assassination of Kaʿb, but he rushed to appeal for the Prophet's mercy and forgiveness upon seeing Islam rise to power. He did so by composing what would become a legendary poem praising the Prophet's ﷺ nobility, using the beautiful language and desert imagery that so moved the Arabs. Not only was the Messenger ﷺ moved by this to forgive him, but he cast upon Kaʿb's shoulders his personal Yemeni cloak, or *burda*, by which name the historic poem became known.[101]

[101] Adapted from *Muhammad: A Very Short Introduction* (pp. 41, 56) by Jonathan A.C. Brown, Oxford University Press, 2011. Also, see: *Sīrah Ibn Hishām* (3/502–512), *Zād al-Miʿād* (3/455) by Ibn al-Qayyim, and *Majmaʿ az-Zawāʾid* (3/407) by al-Haythami, who said therein about at-Ṭabarānī's chain, 'Its narrators until Ibn Ishaq are trustworthy.'

A Flawless Finish

Following the Conquest of Makkah, the Messenger of Allah ﷺ moved to secure the Arabian Peninsula from the lawlessness of the feudal Arab tribes, and from the threat of the neighbouring Byzantine empire. While doing so, he continued his legacy of compassion and forgiveness, leaving as a legacy the best example of ethics and integrity the world has ever seen.

60 A Broken Chief

Mālik ibn 'Awf ؓ was the chief of Hawāzin and, through a large coalition, had mobilized the greatest Arab army ever witnessed to eradicate the Muslims before their strength increased any further. The pagan army was 25,000 strong, and they brought out their wives, children, livestock, and wealth for incentive and morale. It was a horrific confrontation in the valley of Ḥunayn, and the Muslims suffered enormous losses before regrouping to save Islam from extinction.

After the dust cleared, Mālik ibn 'Awf was among those who escaped to the fortresses of Thaqīf (a coalition member) in Ṭā'if, having lost everything. When he was in this broken and desperate state, the Messenger of Allah ﷺ was still thinking about him. When he ﷺ was informed that he was alive, and had taken cover in the fortresses out of fear for his life, he said, 'Inform Mālik that if he comes to me as a Muslim, I will return his family and wealth to him, and will give him [beyond that] a hundred camels.'[102]

[102] Collected by at-Ṭabarī in *Tārīkh al-Umam wal-Mulūk* (2/174)

Is this the expected reaction of a victor to someone he had just defeated? Militaries everywhere find great satisfaction in prosecuting, punishing, and humiliating enemy leaders. To sympathize with and to shower gifts on a defeated enemy is something that most world leaders cannot even comprehend, let alone emulate.

61 The Man from Yā-Sīn

Immediately after the siege of Ṭā'if, 'Urwah ibn Mas'ūd ath-Thaqafi caught up with the Prophet ﷺ before he reached Madinah and asked if he could accept Islam. The Messenger of Allah ﷺ agreed and suggested that 'Urwah not return to his people, saying, 'I fear they will kill you [for becoming Muslim].' 'Urwah did not think so, and said, 'They value me like they value their eyesight, and these people do not even wake me when I am asleep [so how could they lay a hand on me?].'

But upon returning and announcing his Islam, and then making *Adhān al-Fajr* on his roof the next morning, he was killed by archers. In some reports, the Prophet ﷺ said, 'The example of 'Urwah among his people is like that of the man from [*Sūrah*] *Yā-Sīn*; he called his people to Allah and they killed him as a result.'[103]

[103] See: al-Wāqidī (3/960–961).

62 Hypocrites at Tabūk

Fifteen men who had feigned Islam attempted to assassinate the Prophet ﷺ as he rode back from Tabūk. Three of them were killed, and Ḥudhayfah ﷺ was told the names of the remaining twelve. Allah revealed verses exposing them and calling them to repentance.[104] The Prophet ﷺ, despite knowing them by name, chose to warn them of punishment in the world and in the hereafter, saying:

> In my Ummah, there will be twelve hypocrites and they will not be admitted to Paradise and they will not smell its scent until the camel passes through the eye of a needle. An ulcer would be enough [to torment them]; a kind of flame of fire (burning) which would appear in their shoulders and protrude from their chests.[105]

[104] *'They swear by Allah that they did not say [anything against the Prophet] while they had said the word of disbelief and disbelieved after their [pretense of] Islam and planned that which they were not to attain. And they were not resentful except [for the fact] that Allah and His Messenger had enriched them of His bounty. So if they repent, it is better for them; but if they turn away, Allah will punish them with a painful punishment in this world and the Hereafter. And there will not be for them on earth any protector or helper'* (*at-Tawbah* 9:74).

[105] Collected by Muslim (2779)

63 Ibn Salūl's Death

After returning from Tabūk, 'Abdullāh ibn Ubayy died in the ninth year (*hijri*). Despite nearly a decade of direct harm to the Messenger ﷺ and the Muslims, he shrouded this man in his own shirt, prayed over his body, and said, 'Once you are finished [preparing the funeral], inform me.' He came to him after he was lowered in his grave, so he commanded them to remove him. He placed him on his knees and blew into his face. 'Umar رضي الله عنه says:

> When the Messenger of Allah ﷺ stood to pray over him, I jumped towards him and said, 'O Messenger of Allah, are you actually going to pray on Ibn Ubayy, after he has said such-and-such on such-and-such day?' I kept repeating his statements to him, but the Messenger of Allah ﷺ just smiled and said, 'Step back from me, O 'Umar.' When I became excessive in [urging] him, he said, 'I have been given the choice, so I chose [to ask for him to be forgiven]. And had I known that [asking more than] seventy [times] would grant him forgiveness, I would have done more than that.'[106]

[106] Collected by al-Bukhārī (1269) and Muslim (2774)

Imam al-Khaṭṭābī رحمه الله said:

> The only reasons why the Prophet ﷺ did what he did with ʿAbdullāh ibn Ubayy was [because of] his impeccable compassion for those who clung on to any edge of Islam, and to comfort the heart of his son, the righteous man ʿAbdullāh, and to win the hearts of his people (al-Khazraj), since he was their leader.[107]

He also felt indebted to Ibn Salūl for providing his shirt to the Prophet's ﷺ uncle, al-ʿAbbās, after the Battle of Badr, even if it had been done with the wrong intentions.

[107] Cited in *Fatḥ al-Bārī* (8/336)

64 The Man Who Had Him Stoned in Ṭā'if

ʿAbd Yālayl ibn ʿAmr ath-Thaqafi was among the people who inflicted the most pain ever on the Messenger ﷺ. He was the leader of Thaqīf, and the man who ordered that he ﷺ be stoned and run out of the city. For nearly a decade, Thaqīf had resisted Islam's surfacing in Ṭā'if. And, following the conquest of Makkah in the eighth year (*hijri*), they allied with Hawāzin in the Battle of Ḥunayn. And when their ambassador, ʿUrwah ibn Masʿūd ؓ, accepted Islam, they killed him—another devastating blow to the Prophet Muhammad ﷺ.

After the Byzantines fled at Tabūk, Thaqīf realized that the Muslims were now the undisputed power in the Arabian Peninsula. They sent a delegation to Madinah, led by ʿAbd Yālayl, who the Prophet ﷺ received graciously without any mention of their ugly past. He hosted them, furnished them with gifts, and even listened to their demands about accepting Islam on the condition that they be permitted to deal in *ribā*, fornicate, drink wine, not have to pray, and not break the idol of al-Lāt. He discussed these issues with them each night after *ishā'*, in a tent he had erected for them inside the Prophet's Mosque. Ultimately, Islam permeated their hearts, and its Prophet captivated them with his gentleness, and they became one of the greatest strongholds of Islam, even during the apostate wars when rebellions were rampant.

65 A Christian Chief

ʿAdī ibn Ḥātim at-Ṭā'ī felt he had every reason to despise Islam, for he was the chief of Ṭay' (a competing tribe to the Quraysh), as well as a Christian, and an ally to the superpower Byzantium. The father of Kaʿb ibn Ashraf, a warmonger who was executed by the Prophet ﷺ for sedition, was also from Ṭay'. Furthermore, Ṭay' was handily defeated by the Muslim army.

ʿAdī ؓ said, 'When the Messenger of Allah ﷺ was sent, I hated him in a way that surpassed any hatred I have ever had for anything.'[108] After his people were subdued, he roamed the earth as a fugitive, but he eventually became fed up with life and headed to the Prophet ﷺ in Madinah completely unarmed and vulnerable. The Messenger of Allah ﷺ took him in, invited him to Islam, and patiently convinced him of the truth he had brought and the prophecies that would soon come to pass. And thus, this great commander joined the Muslim ranks without hearing any mention of his past, or his war against Islam, or his hatred of its Prophet ﷺ.[109]

[108] Narrated by Ibn Atheer in *Asad al-Ghābah* (3/504) and adh-Dhahabī in *Tārīkh al-Islām* (1/354).

[109] Collected by Ahmad (19397) and al-Arna'oot graded this chain as sound.

66 The Woman Who Poisoned Him ﷺ

Towards the end of his life, the Messenger of Allah ﷺ was invited by a woman from Khaybar, Zaynab bint al-Ḥārith, whose intention was to kill the Prophet ﷺ by poisoning his food! She had prepared a lamb and placed additional poison in the shoulder area which the Prophet ﷺ was known to prefer. He ate from it with his Companions, until revelation informed him that it contained poison. Upon interrogation, Zaynab confessed and admitted, 'I wanted to kill you.' He said, 'But Allah would not enable you against me.' They said, 'O Messenger of Allah, should we not kill her?' He said, 'No' and forgave her. Anas رضي الله عنه says, 'Due to that poison, I continued noticing a mark in [the mouth of] the Prophet ﷺ [until he died].'[110]

[110] Collected by al-Bukhārī (2617) and Muslim (2190); other narrations clarify that he ﷺ initially forgave her for what she did to him, but then handed her fate to the family of Bishr ibn al-Barā' رضي الله عنه who died from her poison, which made them entitled to legal retribution.

67 Musaylamah's Delegates

The tribe of Banū Ḥanīfah enjoyed great strength and a formidable reputation, and they initially accepted Islam like everyone else in Arabia. Upon returning home, they demanded that the Prophet ﷺ show appreciation for their commitment by allotting them leadership after his death. When he ﷺ refused, they renounced Islam and declared Musaylamah al-Ḥanafī (also known as Musaylamah the Imposter) to be their prophet. Despite the audacity of this apostasy and treason, the Prophet Muhammad ﷺ maintained his principles and said to the ambassadors, 'Were it not for the fact that ambassadors are not killed, I would have killed the both of you.'[111] As for Banū Ḥanīfah, they apprehended the Prophet's ﷺ ambassador, Ḥabīb ibn Zayd رضي الله عنه, and cut him to pieces, limb by limb, in front of his family.

[111] Collected by Abū Dāwūd (2761).

Incorruptible

Some Islamophobes have argued that 'Muhammad's changed behaviour and teachings in Madinah are a little too convenient and self-serving for anyone with a grain of skepticism about human nature to swallow.'[112] Although a slight improvement over others' description of the Prophet ﷺ as an opportunist who played possum in Makkah, the view that he was later corrupted by power in Madinah is also plagued by grave fallacies.

Firstly 'Ā'ishah رضي الله عنها, who lived with him ﷺ behind closed doors until his last breath, said:

> Never did the Messenger of Allah ﷺ strike anyone with his hand, neither a servant nor a woman, unless he was fighting in the cause of Allah. He never took revenge upon anyone for the wrong done to him, and would [only] carry out legal retributions for the sake of Allah when the injunctions of Allah were violated.[113]

Ironically, 'Ā'ishah رضي الله عنها lived forty years after the Prophet ﷺ telling the world about his unparalleled ethics, yet it is her narrations that are often twisted by Islamophobes who seek to demonize him.

112 See: *The Enigma of Islam: the Two Faces of Muhammad*, a 'Renew America' article by Fred Hutchison, 30 June 2006.

113 Collected by Muslim (644).

Secondly, desperation can often pose just as much of a challenge to one's integrity as power, and thus we find terrorist groups usually rise out of suppressed political minorities. When people feel that their backs are against the wall and that their disadvantages are suffocating them, that is often when they resort to unethical tactics. Did the Prophet Muhammad ﷺ not witness marginalization and persecution for thirteen years in Makkah and the first few years in Madinah? Yet, he continued to pray for his enemies and to invite them to peace while calming his followers who saw no end in sight to the torture tactics of the Makkans.

Thirdly, the political strength of the Prophet Muhammad ﷺ continued to grow until his death, and we have just seen how his clemency only grew with it. Does not his mercy at the Conquest of Makkah, as just one example, cause the honest skeptic to wonder why power did not lead him to seek revenge against those who slandered him, expelled him, killed his family and followers, and never let up for over twenty years? Would a man consumed by vengeance retain the moral sense to forbid the killing of women, children, monks, the elderly, and non-combatants? Would such a man stop, amidst a military campaign, over a slain woman's body and declare, 'She should not have been harmed'?[114]

To further highlight this last point, it helps to look at people without influence in the Prophet's ﷺ society and times. Even the aggression of the weakest sectors in society was met with

[114] Collected by Abū Dāwūd (2663) and Ahmad (17158).

a similar degree of tolerance by the Prophet Muhammad ﷺ. Nothing can explain why he ﷺ treated even them with such kindness and excellence, other than his sheer magnificence of character, and his passion to save as many souls as possible.

68 The Father of Extremism

While distributing the spoils of war, Dhul Khuwaysirah accused the Prophet ﷺ of dividing them unfairly. He said, ‘Be fair, O Muhammad! For this division [of shares] is not one for which Allah’s face is sought!’ The face of the Prophet ﷺ reflected his anger when he heard this, but he chose to simply reply to this heinous accusation by saying, ‘Woe to you, who would ever be just if I am not just? May Allah bestow mercy upon Moses; he was hurt by more than this and was still patient.’[115] In another narration, ‘You do not trust me, though I am the one trusted by He Who is above the heavens?’

[115] Collected by al-Bukhārī (73/85) and Muslim (1064).

69 Help Him With His Debts

Abū Hurayrah رضي الله عنه reported:

> The Messenger of Allah ﷺ owed a camel of a particular age to a Bedouin man, who demanded it from him in an uncivil manner. This vexed the Companions, and they were about to hurt him, but the Messenger of Allah ﷺ said, 'He who has a right is entitled to speak.' Then he said to them, 'Buy him the camel and give it to him.' They said, 'We cannot find a camel of that age, but found one with a better age than it.' He said, 'Buy that and give it to him, for the best of you are those best in paying off debt.'[116]

[116] Collected by al-Bukhārī (578) and Muslim (3898).

70 The Bedouin Who Suffocated Him

Anas ؓ said:

> I was walking with the Messenger of Allah ﷺ, and he was wearing a Najrānī cloak with a rough collar. A Bedouin man caught up with him, then violently pulled him by his cloak, causing the cloak to tear, and leaving its collar [hanging] on the neck of Allah's Messenger ﷺ. I looked at the Messenger of Allah's ﷺ neck, and the cloak's collar had left marks from how roughly he had snatched [it]. Then, he said, 'O Muhammad, order [them] that I be given from the wealth of Allah that you have!' The Messenger of Allah ﷺ turned to him, smiled, and then ordered that he be given something.[117]

For fourteen centuries, Muslim scholars have deduced from these incidents are not just the hallmarks of good character and forbearance, but understand these to be guidelines for the rulers who followed him ﷺ: that they should be tolerant with their people, endure their physical and financial harm, and overlook any disrespect in order to warm their hearts towards Islam.[118]

---

[117] Collected by al-Bukhārī (3149) and Muslim (1057).

[118] See: *Fatḥ al-Bārī* (10/506) by Ibn Hajar and *Sharh Muslim* (7/147) by an-Nawawī.

A Mercy Misunderstood

Some people find it problematic that, at times, the Prophet ﷺ seems to have stepped outside of his tolerant and forgiving norm. Although analysing each of these 'violent incidents' would be worthwhile, perhaps in another book. We have just illustrated that the Prophet Muhammad ﷺ was undoubtedly inclined to gentleness, forgiveness, and mercy as defaults. However, his mercy did not interfere with his obedience to God, nor the justice that God enjoins. His commitment to mercy was, above all else, a means of devotion to God, and an avenue by which he earned His mercy and pleasure.

For that reason, we find the Prophet ﷺ and Abū Bakr ﵁ weeping from the fear of God: for instance, when He revealed verses after Badr criticizing their decision to 'compassionately spare' the captives. Certainly, this should not be understood to mean that Allah is anti-mercy, for He is the Most Merciful. But it does mean that He is not limited by His mercy. In other words, He knows better that limitless and unconditional mercy is incompatible with other noble values such as justice, and that it does not serve the best interests of humanity. From that perspective, we can begin to understand why the Prophet ﷺ sanctioned the execution of some people, and tactically fought others, though he may have wished that this could have been avoided.[119]

---

[119] The Prophet ﷺ said, "Do not wish to meet the enemy [at war], but when you meet them, stand firm." Collected by al-Bukhārī (2863).

Many times, we as humans—even with good intentions—fail to strike the perfect balance between competing values, and this is just one reason why Allah revealed definitive guidance to help us regulate and contextualize these values.

In the Qur'an, Allah says, *'And when the fright had left Abraham and the good tidings reached him, he began to argue with us concerning the People of Lot. Indeed, Abraham was forbearing, grieving—hurt by human suffering—and [frequently] returning [to Allah].'* (*Hūd* 11:74–75)

Here, God praises Abraham ﷺ as being someone who grieved for human suffering, but also as someone who resigned himself to God's decisions. This was the Prophetic balance that Allah wished to inculcate in the Prophet Muhammad ﷺ through these verses. He did not want His final Prophet to be as heartless as those around him, but neither did He want him ﷺ to adopt a passivity that would result in the merciless becoming brazen and taking advantage of any apparent weakness. The Prophet's ﷺ execution of Abū 'Izzah (the Poet) after Uḥud, after releasing him the previous year without ransom at Badr, is one example of that. He may have wished to forgive him again, for he did forgive others repeatedly, but instead said, 'By Allah, you will not strut in Makkah saying, "I deceived Muhammad twice."'[120]

[120] See: *ar-Rawḍ al-'Unf* (6/30).

Without an external reference point to mediate these values (i.e., divine revelation), the world has disagreed on the boundaries of mercy and justice. Some gravitate to an impractical and utopian extreme, where no forcefulness whatsoever is justified, refusing the reality that some people will never be as 'ethically conscious' as them and will continue transgressing against others unless they are forcefully stopped. Some gravitate to another extreme, using brutality and terror as means to their 'righteous' ends. The majority orbit in the ambiguous middle, each presenting a claim about where a virtue like mercy ends and where another like justice begins. Just as a rusted coin will not be polished by a gentle scrub, some souls require a degree of 'harshness' to remedy them. And just as surgical amputation is generally avoided, but is sometimes a necessary last resort to save a life, sometimes mercy is embodied in sacrificing some lives to save many more.

We hope and pray that these seventy incidents, paraphrased for the sake of conciseness, serve as a reminder of who the Prophet ﷺ really was: a man of mercy and moral greatness who sought not the praise of this world, but its betterment through his example. May God's endless peace and blessings be upon him, his family, his Companions, and those who follow in their blessed path.

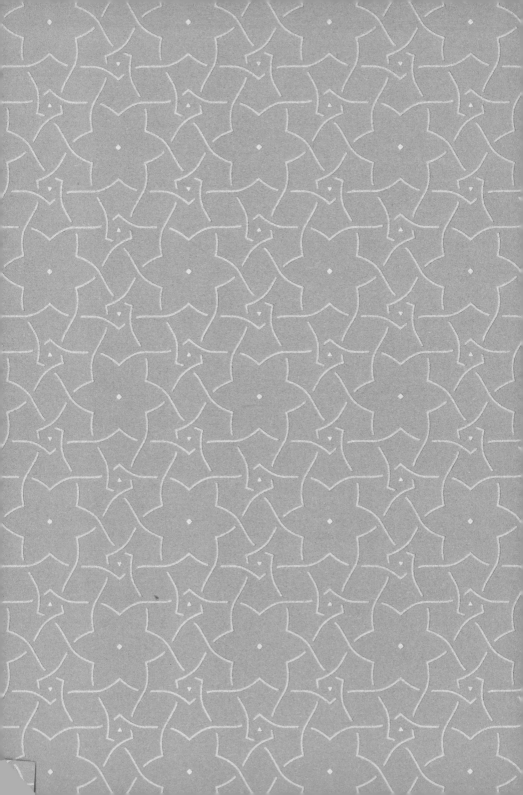